This Is My Life

Malcolm Morris

Virgin

First published in Great Britain in 1996 by
Virgin Books
an imprint of Virgin Publishing Ltd
332 Ladbroke Grove
London W10 5AH

A catalogue record for this book is available from the British Library.

ISBN 1 85227 599 5

Typeset by TW Typesetting, Plymouth, Devon
Printed and bound in Great Britain by
Mackays of Chatham Ltd, Chatham, Kent.

For my darling Anna, Manuela and Gregory,
and my good friend Michael Aspel – never forgetting
Grainne and Eamonn Andrews.

Contents

Illustrations

All photographs from author's collection and Thames Television

An early study of me taken by my Aunt Rose
With my mother, Jessie Morris, 1962
Lewis Morris – my father
With my mother again
On honeymoon with Anna in the Bahamas, 1969
In New York with Eamonn and his wife, Grainne, 1975
My daughter, Manuela, 1992
On holiday in Spain with my son, Gregory, 1995
Filming at Tyne Tees TV with Des O'Connor, 1959
Muhammad Ali, me, Lucille Ball, Eamonn Andrews and Noel
    Coward, 1965
With The Duke of Edinburgh after his first live TV appearance,
    1968
With Zsa Zsa Gabor, 1964 . . .
. . . and again in 1992
With Liz Dawn, *Coronation Street*'s Vera Duckworth, 1995
With Pierce Brosnan and Michael Aspel in 1995, plotting a 'hit' on
    Desmond Llewellyn – 'Q' in the James Bond movies
With Ursula Andress, 1993
Buzz Aldrin, 1994
Bob and Delores Hope, 1995
Jane Russell, 1995
In Hollywood with King Kong, 1989
Rehearsing with my son, Gregory, who's standing in for our next
    subject, William Shatner, 1989
Michael dressed as Sooty, poised to surprise Harry Corbett, 1988
Michael getting into character for a 'hit' on Charlie Drake, 1995
With Margaret Thatcher, recording a message for Jimmy Young,
    1985 . . .

... and with her *Spitting Image* clone in Montreux, 1989

With John Major, recording a message for cricket umpire Dickie Bird, 1992

With Chaim Herzog, President of Israel, 1985

With Shimon Peres, Prime Minister of Israel, 1985

Eamonn clutching a red accounts book ready to pounce on Bill Roache, *Coronation Street*'s Ken Barlow, 1985

Scheduling the running order for the 1994/95 series

Achieving a childhood ambition – sitting in a Spitfire, 1993

Stalking David Hasselhoff on the set of *Baywatch*, 1993

Revisiting old haunts, 1995

Foreword

by Michael Aspel

In 1988, one of the things that persuaded me to take on the job of presenting *This Is Your Life* – apart from the power and the glory – was the personality of producer Malcolm Morris. He made the idea sound interesting, worthwhile and fun, while at the same time warning me that it could be frustrating, exhausting, and as demanding as any over-possessive mother.

He was right on all counts.

His understanding of the reasons behind the appeal of the 'Life' – of what it should always be and what it must never be allowed to become – has been instrumental in the show's enduring popularity. The bonus in all this was that Malcolm and I soon became firm friends. We are the same age, come from similar backgrounds, and have shared interests.

To the rest of the team we are a quaint old couple of film and car buffs, passing our declining years in querulous disputes about who played who in which silent movie, and whether the 300 ZX or the RX7 makes a nicer noise. He will, of course, deny my superior knowledge in all departments, but it is the daily stimulation of trying to outwit me that keeps him young. Being a contemporary of Malcolm means that I can empathise with all his youthful struggles and conquests, and appreciate his shrewd comments on the comings and goings in television.

He has, as you will learn, seen it all and done most of it. Read, enjoy.

Prologue

L os Angeles, 12.35 p.m., 25 October 1989. From the
30th floor of the office complex you could see from
Beverly Hills to Santa Monica. It was a very hot but
crystal clear day in mid-town Los Angeles. Time was running out and the aides began looking at their watches to
show everybody that it had to be this take or nothing.

I got into my position, picked up the scroll and watched
ex-President Ronald Reagan getting ready. The red light
went on, the auto-script was prepared. A nervous sound
man, sweating with tension, tried to attach a small radio
microphone on to the ex-President's tie, but it kept slipping
out of his moist fingers. An aide cleared his throat loudly.
The microphone was fixed at last, the sound man tested it
and with a deep sigh of relief gave a thumbs up.

'Mr President, we really should be going,' the aide said.

'Mr President' shrugged. We would go on, but the aide
had made his point. We had to get this take and I was about
to play a strange role with the ex-President of the United
States of America.

We were in the ex-President's Los Angeles office. A large
flag of the Stars and Stripes was on one wall with the American Eagle standing on a pillar at its side. What was a Blitz
kid from Islington, North London, doing here with the man
who had just been the most powerful person in the world?
He looked at me and gave me a small wink. I blushed, something I had not done for at least, well, I couldn't remember.

'Action.' The cue was given and I went into action. I moved closer to the ex-President and held out the scroll for him to accept. He moved into the shot with ease – he had done this sort of thing before – and accepted the scroll with a dazzling smile.

'Thank you, Margaret,' he said, and took the scroll from me.

I blushed again.

He then went into his speech to the camera and when it was over, he shook my hand and disappeared.

I had just represented the Prime Minister of Great Britain, Mrs Margaret Thatcher.

What was that all about? Read on!

1 Earliest Memories

Nothing much happened in 1932 except that Mr and Mrs Earhart's daughter Amelia became the first pilot to fly alone across the Pacific, a young chap called Adolf Hitler held a successful rally in Germany, the United States of America decided not to recognise the new revolutionary government of Russia, and Mr G. Palmer of Wood Green advertised in *The Times* that his one-year-old Rolls Royce, a gleaming de luxe model, was for sale at £650.

Altogether a rather boring year really, but not for me. I was born at 12.30 p.m. on 29 August in that very year. Only ten days later I was invited to a cheese and wine party. I was the guest of honour and to prove it a small sponge filled with red wine was pressed against my ten-day-old lips. This is the life, I must have thought, and I must have been happy until a hand reached down, took out my ten-day-old manhood, and sliced the top off.

What lessons were there to be learnt that day?

First, never trust a party invitation where you are the guest of honour and second, always expect the worst when you are at your happiest.

After that I recall very little of my early life. I remember being balanced on the shoulder of my Aunt Rose for a photograph. I was about two years old and only remembered the moment when many years later I saw a creased and broken photograph on the page of a family photo album. I remember being taken on her shoulder into the concrete yard at the back of our house that was above the hairdressing shop that my parents owned. That back yard was no more than 25 feet square, with brick walls at each end and bound on either side by a butcher and a furniture shop, but for a while it became my universe.

We lived at 335 Caledonian Road in North London but I was born in my grandmother's house a mile further along the same road. My granny was a Scot from Ayr and did not like the English or my mother, but she liked me. She had a house with a garden at the posh end of Caledonian Road, or 'the Cally', as it was called by the natives at the time. A little further from her house on the left was the Holloway Prison for women – a solemn, mysterious castle – and a mile along 'the Cally' on the right was Pentonville, the hanging prison with its terrifying six foot thick walls.

Being born between these two monuments to justice was a sober encouragement to a life on the straight and narrow. Such encouragement, however, was not needed by me when, as a five year old, I played my games in my concrete 25 foot square universe. I can't say if we were poor because I'm not sure any more what poor or rich is. I can only say that I now know people whose lifestyles vary from rented rooms to several houses in different parts of the world. I also know that there are people who would envy the rented room and also some who would look down upon those with the worldwide accommodation. I do know that we were a working-class Jewish family who did not follow the religion in that Saturday was a working day with eggs and bacon for breakfast.

My parents, Jessie and Lewis Morris, ran the hairdressing shop called 'Maison Morris' which catered for men and women, my Grandad Barney running the gents side and my father doing both. My mother worked in the ladies part of the salon and was very popular with her customers who came in for a 'wash and set' for 3/6d and maybe an occasional perm for 12/6d, but it wasn't just their hair that was teased at the salon as they were bombarded with a non-stop cabaret of one-liners by my mother. Woody Allen would have been proud of some of my mother's gags.

I was happy and was about to learn my first lesson – at the moment when you say to yourself 'I'm happy', that's when it all changes.

The changes began one morning when I was washed, dressed, polished and fed with a large bowl of hot, sugary porridge. Wrapped in my overcoat I was taken by my father on a long walk. Fifteen minutes later we reached the huge brick walls that surrounded Laycock Street State School. We went in. I looked at the glass doors and I could smell old dust and that special odour that can only come from 150 children. My father told me that this was the new school we had talked about for so long. That was news to me, for as far as I remembered, we had never talked about it. I do remember saying, however, that it was all right to leave me and that I would not cry – and I didn't. It wasn't until that night when I was told I would be going back again the next morning that it really hit me.

One day was OK, but for ever . . .

I cried and cried and then I started to negotiate: what if I read books at home? Just to make the deal even more attractive to my parents I threw in that I would also go to bed early.

No deal. Nothing worked, and the following day off I went, only this time clutching a small brown Woolworths satchel with a set of colouring pencils and some picture books.

Laycock Street School was a fairly typical North London state school: rough, tough and uncompromising. I learnt quickly that the class was divided into gangs, and although nothing happened for the first few weeks, within a month I was a little veteran of avoiding being beaten up.

I had managed to acquire a pair of roller skates. They were made of metal and were attached to each shoe by two front metal lugs that when tightened gripped on to the sole of the shoe.

I could skate the journey to school on my own in about ten minutes, unclip each skate, hide them in the school yard and in I would go.

I had formed friendships with some bigger lads who would protect me if I was threatened in any way, but when that failed, I was off on my skates like a flash.

One weekend I was taken to my mother's parents who lived in Bow in the East End of London. There I met my grandfather, a six foot four giant with red hair and a large red moustache. He picked me up and as I stared up at him he spoke to me, but I couldn't understand a word he was saying, which was not surprising really because he was speaking Russian! I began to panic so he switched to Yiddish, and that really did it. He put my wriggling body down and I ran across the room and hid behind a large armchair. I could just about cope with the Scottish accents of my other grandparents but this was too much for a North London lad. My Russian grandmother was tiny with a kind wrinkled face, but she spoke only in Yiddish and I didn't know what the hell she was saying to me. I strained my ears and stared into her face, and I asked my dad why she didn't speak English. My father told me that he couldn't understand her either because his parents were Scottish.

He went on to tell me that my mother's parents had come from a tiny village on the Russian–Polish border called Klimashlovnitzia, and that my grandfather was once a Cossack.

'Why are they in London?' was a question I remember asking.

'Because the Jews had to leave Russia,' I was told.

'Why?'

'Because they were Jews.'

'So?'

'Well, they would have been badly treated or put in prison if they had stayed.'

'Why are they Jews?'

'Because they are.'

I looked at my dad. 'But your mum and dad are from Scotland so they're not Jews.'

'Yes they are. And so are you.'

I remember looking into a mirror and thinking, I'm in deep trouble.

Nothing had changed yet I was now different, and I went back to school knowing that nobody else there was the same as me. Nothing happened, however; the same boys tried to catch me and give me a thumping for the same old reasons. Life went on the same as always.

September arrived. The year was 1939. I remember another burning hot afternoon on my aunt's balcony. She lived in Brighton and I was enjoying the sea breeze while reading *Doctor Dolittle Goes to the Moon*. I was suddenly aware that my mother was crying because my father was going back to London without us. There was a 'war'. In the end we followed him a week later. My one thought about the war was whether or not I could negotiate a delay in going back to school. These patriotic hopes were dashed when my mother told me to get ready because she was taking me to an outfitters to get a new school cap.

My school did not have an emblem, so my mother chose a cap with a particularly dramatic design which I hated on sight. She was in no mood for debate, however, and it ended in tears.

When we got back home in London I rushed to fetch a newspaper and placed my cap next to the photos on the front page, showing both to my mother.

'Now do you agree that it's not for me?' I asked.

The emblem on my cap was a Swastika!

My mother was not to be defeated; it had been an expensive cap and she believed nobody would notice or remember the emblem after a few weeks. I gave up the argument, but began to have nightmares of being the only Jewish boy in Laycock Street School to turn up on the first week of the war wearing a cap with a Swastika emblazoned on the front. My duty was clear. I quietly went out and placed the cap carefully on the tramlines outside our house and watched with triumph as the number 517 tram gently, neatly and with great efficiency, cut the cap in half. It meant a hell of a wallop, but it was worth it and for me it marked the beginning of the war.

2 War

C ountless books have been written about World War II, but for me there was nothing historic going on. For me, the war was a matter of netting being stuck across all the windows in all the streets and a high metal post with a siren on top being erected across from our house.

Much more personal was the hole that was dug in my back yard. My concrete universe was violated by a domed corrugated iron hut known for some obscure reason as an Anderson shelter. It was about eight feet wide by ten feet long with a concrete floor. A few luxuries were soon added to it, such as a thick wooden door, two sets of wooden bunk beds, a small electric light and an electric fire. The light and fire were both connected by cable to the house and were probably both quite lethal in the event of any bomb blast baring the cable against the corrugated iron. It was, however, the least harmful of things that threatened us. We were being bombed and blitzed by high explosives, incendiaries, phosphorus bombs, landmines and razor sharp shrapnel fragments from exploding anti-aircraft shells. I remember feeling that a lot of nasty people were doing their very best to kill me, yet in spite of everything, my world was very exciting. Although most of the children were evacuated to the countryside, my parents had made the decision that we would stay and live or die together, so I lived through the war in blitzed and bombed London.

Another novelty for me was our air-raid siren which

would sound a wavering note for just over a minute to warn of an impending air raid. I negotiated a deal with my mother which allowed me to go out on my roller skates – provided I could return before the siren had finished. This meant that the perimeters of my play area were as wide as my ability to skate back to the house before the end of the siren. It was a challenge not to be missed and I became lightning on wheels.

London during the Blitz was a vast playground for those children not evacuated. Bombed buildings and large craters became wonderful places to explore. Especially attractive were the dangerous and sinister craters that were marked DANGEROUS UNEXPLODED BOMB – DO NOT EN-TER. These – naturally – were the favourites of any dare that was going at the time. How far would you go into the crater before you gave in to your fear?

Many would go in and come out fast, saying that they had seen a vast black bomb with Swastikas on it, but nobody ever believed them. The real trade was to be found in shrapnel, which could be quite lucrative as an exchange for American comics, and if you were lucky to have a jagged piece with markings on, well, you were in for a piece of unused chewing gum as well.

My collection of comics and shrapnel grew until I found the ultimate status symbol: a twelve inch long green silk plaid rope. German landmines were dropped in by parachute so that they would explode 100 feet in the air before impact and thus do a lot of widespread damage. My rope was part of such a parachute. I still get annoyed to this day when I think of my mother actually throwing it away after the war. Perhaps it was her revenge for my sliced school cap!

A short way along the Caledonian Road, past Pentonville Prison and just before the Caledonian market, was my 'real' world. It centred around the Mayfair, which was the best cinema in existence. It showed three different programmes a week and I would usually go three times a week. I always went twice with my mother, on Mondays and Thursdays.

Saturday mornings were different; I would take an apple, spit on it, polish it to a high gloss and take it to a cinema in King's Cross which always showed the latest *Flash Gordon* serials. I would sit staring at the blank screen, trembling with excitement while waiting for the film to start. If only I had known then that I would actually meet 'Flash' in person some 40 years later – but that's another story!

I would round off the week on Sunday afternoons by going back to the Mayfair, where I would sit in breathless anticipation for the following week's trailers, which ran for over twenty minutes. They were always my favourite part of the Sunday programme. I was obsessed with Bogart, Cagney, Raft and Edward G. Robinson, and the Bob Hope and Bing Crosby *Road* films were just sheer magic. I wonder what I would have said if I had been told then that I would meet them all one day?

I remember all the films I saw at that time and I can also remember the actual scenes, and the way in which each one was shot. A camera angle would stay in my mind in greater detail than any school lesson. Sometimes a slide would appear on the screen over the film saying: 'An alert has just gone and an air-raid is now taking place. If you wish to leave the cinema, please keep your ticket and you will be allowed back at no extra charge.' Nobody ever moved. Life went on, and so did the films.

By the time I was ten, it was 1942 and the Blitz was increasing in intensity, yet my life was set in a fixed pattern. My father was too old for the forces so he became a special reserve policeman on night duty. He would run the shop during the day, sleep a bit in the early evening, and go on duty at about ten o'clock at night. 'Maison Morris' would close at about six o'clock, and each evening we would go into our Anderson shelter as a matter of course. A little later we were to indulge in even more elaborate precautions. A friend had given my parents their reservation of two bunk beds at Piccadilly underground station, which was one of the deepest in London. At six each evening we would catch a number fourteen bus to Piccadilly Circus and would arrive in central London at about seven p.m., just before the first raid of the evening was sounded. We would then make our way down the steps into the underground station.

Our two bunk beds were in the middle of the platform, beside the wall which bore the plaque 'Piccadilly Circus'. I spent many hours trying to remove the enamel 'Y' from the sign. It was my ambition to see 'Piccadill' on that wall as my contribution to the war effort.

Further along the line of bunks was Edna Littlewood, a rounded twelve year old girl with reddish hair and a permanent scowl. She had a top bunk and I remember going past her with careful timing so as to catch her sitting on the side with her plump legs dangling over the edge. The object, of course, was to see up her skirt, but the light in the underground was so bad that this vision was not to be mine. One night I told Edna that I had discovered a secret way into Swan and Edgars, the big store above the station and did she want to come and see? She did, so off we went. I took her through a connecting doorway into the basement floor of the store and I remember that all the counters were covered up for the night while the dim night lights from the street gave the whole place a mysterious glow. Encouraged by my companion, I decided to explore further and so we made our way through the carpeted passages. Edna Littlewood suddenly made a decision and stopped dead in her tracks. She looked at me intently and asked whether I would like to put my hand up her skirt. Would Billy Bunter have liked another pie? Would Just William have liked 100 conkers? Would Sexton Blake have wanted to catch a spy? No German land-mine could have shocked me more than that question, which I could not answer other than to nod my head in a very positive way. I eventually asked her when this could take place. 'Oh, anytime you like,' she replied. She was walking slowly between the covered counters so I went up behind her and did just as she suggested.

With that first exploration I turned a corner in my life. I wonder where Edna Littlewood is today? Did she survive the war? Did she go on to bigger things? Dear Edna, of that generous soul, if you are out there, you are now knocking on 65. I raise my glass to you. It will be the second thing I have raised to you in my life.

3 ... and Peace

Two great events took place in 1945. One was the end of the war and the other was my Barmitzvah. I shall deal with the most dramatic one first.

A Barmitzvah is a Jewish ritual which requires a boy of thirteen to take part in a religious ceremony to mark that he has become a man. The ceremony takes place in a synagogue and the newly made 'man' is required to sing a passage from the Bible entirely in Hebrew. To ensure the event is completely traumatising, it takes place in front of his entire family and friends, which is fine if you're Al Jolson. I was and still am a basically shy person who avoids putting himself into highly visible public situations. The very thought of this ceremony even today can put a rash of goosepimples across my back, but in 1945 it positively terrified me.

Two years earlier I had arrived at the first of the Sunday sessions with the Rabbi who was to teach me to read and speak Hebrew. At the time I was a student at St Aloysius, a Catholic college in Highgate which was run by the Christian Brothers.

Hebrew is written, read and, for all I know, spoken backwards from right to left. Hebrew books opened at the end which I would close. I was already at the bottom of my class for English, French and Latin and was busy trying to speak Yiddish to my Russian grandmother who, by this time, was living with us. I needed another language like the Luftwaffe needed more Spitfires.

On the first Sunday the Rabbi asked me to sing a few notes and on hearing the sound issuing from my mouth, said that although the scriptures decreed that the holy passages should be sung, he would make an exception in my case and that I could just read them out aloud. Whether this was to safeguard Jewish ritual, avoid offending the Almighty or merely saving the Rabbi's sanity, I will never know. For the next two years I felt physically sick whenever calculating the diminishing time to 29 August 1945, the day of my Barmitzvah.

It came and I decided that it was going to be such a disaster that I would leave my body and watch the whole day quite safely from on high. I switched off and observed quite objectively, knowing that whatever happened on the day would eventually finish.

I stood there on the raised centre in the synagogue, watched intently by my mum and dad, my Uncle Sam and Aunt Marie and my cousins Harold, June and Anita, as well as my Aunt Lilly, Uncle Maurice and Pamela, my attractive younger cousin, who years earlier played the nurse to my inevitable role as doctor. The rest of my family was there as well. All were trying to keep straight faces. I looked down on me, looking glazed in front of the Hebrew Scriptures. I saw with interest how my bone dry mouth opened and out came my right to left voice. I didn't have the faintest idea what I was saying but everyone seemed reasonably pleased and nobody laughed out loud in the middle. At the end the Rabbi shook my hand. 'Muzzeltov' he said. He was happy, I suspect, out of the sheer joy of knowing that he would probably never see me again . . . and he was right.

In order to have arrived at my Barmitzvah it follows that I had survived the war, but that was no thanks to Hitler, who I believe did his honest best to help me to miss 1945 altogether. He bombed me from 1941 with a night-and-day Blitz that on one occasion reached spectacular heights which when seen from the top window of our house, seemed to have placed a fireball across the London horizon. Looking at that scene I knew that I was watching history in action.

Many years later I met Air Vice Marshal 'Johnnie' Johnson, DSO, DFC, the wonderful and well-decorated fighter pilot who had led a Spitfire Squadron in the Battle of Britain. I told him that I had been only five thousand feet below one of his triumphant dog fights.

Yet nothing the war had produced had really touched me until the day I grew up. That was the day I saw the first pictures of Belsen and Auschwitz. Nothing in my life had prepared me for the impact of those terrible photographs of the starving and the dying and the mounds of dead bodies from the concentration camps. I realised that those people were Jews; I heard again my father's words, 'and so are you', and I realised that if I had been born on the other side of the Channel, all my family could have been part of those scenes. Up to that moment the war for me had been a glorious adventure, but from then on it became real and horrible.

On one wonderful day in May 1945 my mother and father took me on a walk of many miles from North London to Piccadilly, but I don't think I saw the ground for the last two miles because of the crowds of people packed on the pavements. It was VE Day, and the war in Europe was over.

I have already mentioned that I now attended St Aloysius, a Catholic college run by the Christian Brothers. I hear you ask, 'What's a nice Jewish boy doing in a Catholic school?' The answer is not found in some divine conversion, but in our family's eight-by-ten foot Anderson shelter. During one particularly bad air-raid some years earlier, my mother and I were in the Anderson shelter when my father arrived home at the end of his night duty as a policeman. He came to see if we were all right as there had been some heavy bombing very close to us. As he spoke, another close explosion shook the ground and took out most of the windows in our house. That was when my father began to argue with my mother on the merits of all of us being in the countryside. After all, he had a family in Scotland we could go to.

My mother disagreed and I remember very clearly that I looked up from my bunk bed and also disagreed, but I went a little further and told my father to fuck off.

Even in the midst of tons of explosives falling all around us, there followed an amazing silence as they both stopped dead and my father slowly turned to me. Before his disbelief could turn to anger, my mother explained that it was something that I had heard at school and didn't really understand. Looking at my father's face, I nodded in quick agreement. The week before my parents had discovered eight 1942 Woolworths diaries in my bedroom which I had obviously pinched, and this was the last straw. They decided it was imperative that I changed my school as soon as possible before I took up permanent residence in Pentonville.

St Aloysius came highly recommended as a school with very strict emphasis placed on discipline. The Christian Brothers were not Jesuits, but were no amateurs in the field of discipline either. I loved it, and I got on very well with all the brothers. In turn they were all very nice to me, the only Jew in the place. Maybe they viewed me as some sort of Catholic penance!

There was one exception to the teaching brothers and that was the English teacher, Mr Smith. He was a layman and I don't know why he was there unless it was for the express purpose of terrifying me. Mr Smith had a Heinrich Himmler-style haircut, and wore inevitable frameless glasses. He looked to me as if he came straight out of a Conrad Veidt Warner Bros. film, but without the happy ending. My mind went blank whenever I saw him, I learnt nothing and quickly went to the bottom of the class.

I eventually resorted to my special technique of crawling; it had never failed me before. 'Mr Smith, I don't think I'm doing very well. Perhaps you can give me some additional homework?'

It didn't work. He slammed his hand down hard on his desk and I jumped in the air with fright. I didn't fool him one little bit; I was a slacker, he said, and I was not going to get around him by that pathetic ruse. He pushed his glasses tighter into his face and leaned closer to me, telling me that in future he would be watching me very carefully.

I learnt two things that day I have never forgotten.

First, never underestimate your enemy and second, there is nothing more painful than a con that doesn't work.

The rest of my time at school was spent happily and because of my loner instincts and dislike of most team sports, I avoided all games. I did relent on two occasions, the first time when I was persuaded to take part in a cricket match. St Aloyius was noted for its excellent team. I was placed in the position called 'silly mid on', and I found out why it was called that when I found myself placed only a few feet from a very powerful batsman. He, of course, gave the first ball an enormous whack straight at me. In shock I put my hands in front of my face, the ball went rocketing into my hands, he was out and I had almost broken my little finger. I resigned from cricket from that very moment and have happily not played or watched it since.

Next, I tried football. This time I watched a few matches carefully beforehand, and decided that the safest and therefore the best position to be in was that of goalie and so that's where I found myself. The match began and unfortunately, but perhaps inevitably, someone kicked the ball at my goal. I dived in just the way I had seen others do – they had sort of flown across the soft grass to catch the ball and save the day. My dive, however, was different; for one thing, I didn't reach the ball, and for another, the soft grass wasn't soft at all. My landing seemed to crack every rib in my body. I resigned from the game immediately and have never had the urge to play it ever again.

At about this time I was given a box camera, which started my great love of photography. Mr Smith would have been amazed at the books that I learnt from; I absorbed volumes about lenses, processing, composition and art. My photography was to stand me in better stead than any lesson I ever learnt at school. Photography complemented my obsession for the cinema, but how to direct these talents? I was now fourteen years old, matriculation loomed ahead while the war and my Barmitzvah were now firmly in the past.

What to do now?

4 Skyliner

had realised by my early teens that to continue at school would be a waste of everybody's time, so I grabbed the chance that was suggested by my father.

Why not go into hairdressing! It didn't require any spelling, History or English, and you could run your hands through any girl's hair and get paid for it. It sounded like just the job for me. A young Howard Keel had just starred in a new musical called *Oklahoma!* and I was humming one of its songs as I made my way once again to Piccadilly Circus, only this time it was not to dodge the bombs but to enrol at the Morris International School of Hairdressing, run by award-winning hair stylist André Morris.

Mr 'André' was no relative of mine, and I doubt whether his real name was 'André', but he was a very good hairdresser, and I took to the course as well as the proverbial duck to setting lotion.

Six months later, being able to Marcel wave, razor cut, perm and style hair, I was ready to take on the world. Determined not to work at 'Maison Morris', I set my sights on the West End of London and was offered a job through the school even before I had finished the course. Mr André had done his stuff, and it was the first of the many opportunities that were to come my way. The fact is that to this day I have never actually applied or been interviewed for a job and I'm almost ashamed to say that I have not been unemployed for as long as one day since I left the terrifying Mr Smith and the wonderful Christian brothers.

The West End hairdresser where I went to work was called Guerney and it had a very exclusive clientele from nearby Hampstead and St John's Wood. Now, every Londoner will know that Hampstead could not by any stretch of the imagination be called the West End of London, but in hairdressing parlance, that was its area. I only mention this because that type of client was very important to a hairdresser: the area and its snob value would dictate the sort of styling that I would do and get paid for accordingly. Within one year I had the 'chutzpa', or cheek, to give a demonstration of advanced hairstyling at a hairdressing convention called the 'Silver Rose Bowl' and I received a very good press notice, which wasn't bad for a sixteen year old!

I have kept the press cutting to this day to show any disbelievers.

Looking back, I believe that the 1950s were the most formative years of my life. My parents bought me a new car for my eighteenth birthday. It was a light blue Austin A30, a baby car with two doors and a pair of flapper arms for indicators. It was wonderful, my pride and joy, and now I was mobile and the world had grown just that little bit smaller. The car arrived at just the right moment in my life, as now my pursuit of a good social life was reaching desperate levels. By that I mean that I was determined to lose my virginity; I just had to find out what all the fuss was about – and this was not easy in the pre-pill fifties.

My happy hunting grounds were the four main dance halls in London; the Lyceum in the Strand, the Astoria and the Paramount in Tottenham Court Road and the frantic Hammersmith Palais.

The ritual was always the same. Working by myself, I would usually start at the Lyceum and walk around the tables at the back of the dance floor. I would then go up to the balcony and just watch the dancers for about fifteen minutes. Mimicking Alan Ladd, I would then casually reach for my Lucky Strike cigarettes, light up and contiue to study the form, as he would have done. Although I could dance quite well, the difficult part came when I saw a girl I wanted to dance with. The ritual was always the same and could be embarrassing because the girls mostly stood in small groups, eyeing up the boys. The approach could only be made head-on in front of everybody else, and there was no other way to do it; I just had to go up to her, stand there, look into her eyes and ask her. I was then at the girl's mercy. She would usually pause, look me up and down, look at her friends and then look back to deliver the verdict. No prisoner has ever been studied more closely by his hanging judge.

Life could be difficult for a teenage boy in 1950.

The music was also very important; if it was the wrong tempo then you would be dead. Charlie Barnet's 'Skyliner' would demand good jiving talents by you and your partner. A special Joe Loss version of 'In the Mood' or 'In a Persian Market' would always move things briskly along. But if the gods were smiling down on you, and the girl complete in her tight Lana Turner sweater would say the magic word, 'Yes' or even a mumbled, 'OK', then you were in. Then after all that, if the band went into the smooth Glen Miller 'Moonglow' or 'Blue Moon', you had it made.

Life, however, always has some surprises in store just when you're not expecting them. Joe Loss was playing a very slow number at the Astoria when I asked Elizabeth to dance and not only did she say 'yes' but that she would 'love to'. That sort of response is very good for the confidence and I was particularly smooth that night. We got on so well that she agreed to come with me on the next Saturday night to Southend, and what's more, we agreed to stay the night!

Nobody ever approached a weekend with more imaginative plans and more fear than I had that week. Would she change her mind? She didn't. Did she really say that we would come back on the Sunday? She did, and before I knew it we were at the Bella Vista Hotel in Southend and I was looking the landlady straight in the face, asking for a bed and breakfast for one night.

The die was cast and the evening and night were ours, so first we went to dinner and then on to the local Mecca dance hall and had a few gin and tonics. Then it was time for the suave man of the world to deliver the goods.

I was a disaster and I was still 'intacto' the following morning, facing a very puzzled young lady. I could only bluff it out, so suggested breakfast quite casually. 'Just remember to act as though we're married,' I advised. We sat, as fate would have it, at the one breakfast table that was in the centre of the room so was under the scrutiny of all the more mature weekenders. The waiter served up the breakfast but forgot the sugar.

'Shall I bring some, Sir?'

I looked at Elizabeth. 'Do you take sugar?' I asked. The silence was only broken by a muffled snigger.

Elizabeth was a nurse who worked and lived at the Tottenham Royal Hospital and I took her back on Sunday morning. She invited me up to her room, out of pity, I supposed. Reluctantly I parked my baby car and we went up. With no planning, scheming or thinking, we somehow went straight to bed and lo and behold, I lost my cherry!

Dear, sweet Elizabeth, here's to you wherever you are. I may not have been your best lover, but at least I made you laugh!

5 Somebody's Mother

I was happy with my life, which is, as I've said before, always a dangerous state to be in. Then out of the blue my father had a suspected heart attack and I had no choice but to leave my job in the West End and run 'Maison Morris' with my mother. Although he recovered, I couldn't leave them alone, so I began working in Caledonian Road, doing hair cutting, perms, dyeing and setting which had to last for two weeks or there would be big complaints.

I knew that's what I had to do, but it wasn't for me and I became bored with the day to day work. Two years earlier at hairdressing training school, I had met up with Leon Sykes, who had also just joined and by coincidence lived very near to me. We became great pals and decided to do photographic jobs on the side.

He would manage the business side and I would take the pictures – weddings, baby pictures and anything else we could get our hands on. All this was going on while we were both working at our day jobs.

Things looked up when Leon got us a very big contract to cover an expensive wedding. We were to photograph the wedding and provide an album of about 25 pictures for £15 30s, plus we could take pictures of the guests for extra money. He did warn me, however, that these people were very fussy and there must be no mistakes.

It all went very well. I shot everything and everybody while Leon took notes of every photograph. The focus of the evening, like most weddings, was the cutting of the cake, and my flash gun worked and that was fine.

Except that much later that night in my dark and musty basement underneath the hairdressing shop I began to examine the negatives. I couldn't believe it – the 'cutting of the wedding cake' had an extra irony. I had cut off all the heads in the picture and I had not taken a second one.

Now I knew why photographers always said, 'Just one more!'

We both stared at the headless torsos in horror. Our photo business was finished.

'Wait a minute,' I said. 'I can enlarge the couple's head from other pictures, stick them on, and rephotograph the doctored picture. They will never know,' I reassured my distraught partner.

And so it was. All that night I rephotographed and processed and stuck things together, and as dawn broke I gave the last photo to him.

Leon delivered the album and collected the money. The only puzzled question came from the bride's mother, who wondered why she wasn't in the 'cake' photo as she had been standing behind her daughter at the time.

As I was still working in the hairdressing shop I also began to do some arty styles at the local hairdressing academy and then I would photograph them. I began to disappear more and more into my musky darkroom next to the coal cellar. I used a biscuit tin as an enlarger and Leon and I called our photographic company 'Personality Photographs', which was duly registered.

I had reached the grand old age of eighteen. I loved photography and I decided to try and get a press card which, protected as it was by a tough union, was probably one of the hardest cards of all to get.

The good thing was, I didn't know it.

I never discovered why John Ware, head of publicity for 20th Century-Fox Films, agreed to see me, but after my telephone call to him I made my way to Soho Square and into his office. This was an efficient man working in an efficient office, so I came straight to the point. I asked him for a pass to cover the big première film launch of *Not as a Stranger* with Robert Mitchum and Loretta Young. I had heard that some very big names were going to be present. He smiled at me; it was an experienced smile to someone who obviously knew nothing. He was, however, very kind, and pointed out that all the agencies would be covering the event and by the time I got back home, their pictures would be running off the newspaper presses.

'What would be the point?' he asked.

Looking him straight in the face, I answered, 'I might get something that they might miss.'

The smile came back, but he took pity on me and signed a pink docket. 'Show that at the door and you'll get in, but you're wasting your time.'

The Odeon, Leicester Square, was decked out with Holly-wood-style searchlights on the roof, although searchlights were no novelty to most Londoners in 1952. This was, how-ever, exciting by anybody's standards; the crowd was huge and flashlights were popping at a fast and furious pace, re-minding me that I was wasting my time. But I was in with my Kodak Retina 11a, Mecablitz flash gun and two dozen tiny flash bulbs that I prayed would flash when required and not explode, which some were inclined to do in those days.

I stalked my prey and came across Gregory Peck. He was a good catch, I decided, so I aimed my camera at him but he was talking to a very old lady. I waved to him and he smiled, then he put his arm around the little old lady who would not stop talking. As he was not going to let her go I took the photograph. No buxom blonde companion, but never mind, the night was still young.

After a few minutes I came across a very nervous Robert Mitchum, but he agreed to pose, so things were looking up for me. As luck would have it the same little old lady came up and gave him a kiss and just stood there talking, so I took the picture anyway and waited for her to go away.

I began to loathe this woman whom I imagined had been sent by the agencies to ruin all my pictures. Robert Mitchum went into the auditorium and I continued my hunt. Straight away I came across the lovely Olivia de Havilland, who was keen for me to take her picture and organised her own pose by a marble column of flowers. I took the picture, thanked her and turned to go, when she called me back. Would I mind taking another one? This time with the woman I hated most in the world; the little old lady who posed with relish and held in front of her the ugliest black handbag I had ever seen in my life.

A waste of time, film and a flashbulb, but I took the photo anyway.

An hour later, deep in my musty black hole, I printed up the pictures. I had debated whether to print the ones with the old witch on because frankly, ten by eight photographic paper was expensive. Then the expediency of hope overcame meanness and I decided to print them all.

John Ware sat at his desk, but all was not the same; the efficiency was somehow diminished. Laid out in front of him were over 100 photographs, all looking very crisp and glossy. My heart sank as he looked up, and I could see that he was a very worried man. I had my own worries too. I opened my envelope and spread my pictures across his desk. The old lady stared up at me from nearly every photo.

His eyes opened wide and he looked through the others. 'How did you know?' he asked, giving me his full attention.

I can't remember my reply but it turned out that the little old lady was the mother of Spyros Skouras, the president of 20th Century-Fox. As luck would have it, the American cable which said she would be present at the première had been delayed, and the foul-up had meant that nobody from the agencies had been briefed to cover her presence for all the trade papers back home in the USA. At that moment, the old lady became the most attractive woman in the world.

I had saved the head of the publicist at 20th Century-Fox and the world was mine. I accepted his heartfelt thanks and asked in return that he provide me with a little press card. He couldn't give it to me personally but he promised he would do his best, and a month later the much coveted press card duly arrived. With that card in my hand I wasted no time and started to cover any big event that I could find.

The biggest event in 1952 was 'The Night of a Hundred Stars' at the London Palladium. My brand-new press card got me through the stage door into the backstage area by the wings. I had never been to the Palladium or indeed any big theatre before, living as I did in my world of the cinema, yet even Alice could not have stepped into a more magical Wonderland.

The walls were covered with ropes and each one was tied to some scenery or to wooden ramps high up on the rook. People swarmed like ants, carrying the fragile sheets of scenery and props, and every time the curtain came down in front of the stage, the music would swell up in volume, the sound of the applause would be deafening, and people would rush on to the stage and dash off again just as the curtain rose to yet more applause. Lights were moving and changing colour, and out of the wings walked Noel Coward, who was compering the show. The lights were intense and directional, so my choice of lighting was either dim shadow or very bright light. Being so close to the stage, using a flash was out of the question – an unforgivable distraction – which is why no other photographers had gone backstage.

I saw that Noel Coward sometimes stayed in the wings between acts so I took a deep breath and asked if I could take some pictures of him. He was a little nervous and perhaps he welcomed this interlude as a way to help calm himself. He told me that since he was wearing a black velvet dinner suit, it would be almost impossible to take a good picture in that light but he thought he knew a way to get around the problem and then went to extraordinary lengths to set up a miniature studio for me.

Between going on stage, he found a rather ornate prop chair and placed it carefully alongside a strong shaft of light which he managed to use as an effect to separate himself from the background. I had recently bought a brand new camera, a Leica 111F that was one of the first out of Germany. It was the Rolls Royce of cameras and he was fascinated by it and the fact that it could work in almost any light. Forgetting that Noel Coward had directed feature films, I was surprised by his technical knowledge. While all this was going on, a tiny, baldheaded man approached me. He told me his name was Ivan Steenburg and that he was a uni-cyclist appearing for the first time in London. He was keen that I should take a picture of him during his act on stage. Being preoccupied with one of the biggest stars in the world, I didn't want to be distracted. I told Ivan Steenburg that I couldn't take his pictures but there were other photographers in the audience who would. However, he wouldn't take no for an answer and was becoming a pest, so I agreed. I finished my pictures of Noel Coward, whom I thanked then and again some twelve years later – but that's another story.

The Palladium pictures came out well and my confidence in my photographic abilities improved as I continued with my hairdressing day job. I couldn't work out where all this was going to lead, but some instinct pushed me on. Two weeks later Ivan Steenburg rang me at the shop to thank me for the photographs and to tell me that he had just been booked for a BBC Television programme called *Café Continental*. He wanted some more pictures of himself at the studios and he wanted me to take them.

I arrived at the BBC Television studios at Lime Grove, Shepherd's Bush on a Saturday night. *Café Continental* was a Saturday night show compered by Père August and a very beautiful lady called Helene Cordet. Ivan was indeed in the show and a pass was waiting for me at reception.

I not only photographed Ivan during rehearsal, but was allowed to photograph the rest of the show. Maurice Chevalier was on the programme, backed by a wonderful Can Can dance routine performed with great abandon by the most energetic and beautiful dancers. The Can Can is one of the most photogenic of all show routines and I took some really spectacular shots of the dance. I then sent them to the show's producer, Henry Caldwell, and a few weeks later he rang me and asked whether I would photograph some more of his programmes. I did, and one week after that, during a very busy hairdressing day, I was to receive a phone call that would change the rest of my life.

6 Fleet Street

Edward Bishop was a tall, rather academic-looking journalist whose ambition had been to start up a television news press agency in Fleet Street. He rang me to say he had seen my *Café Continental* pictures and wanted to employ someone who really knew their way around a television studio. He asked if I would consider joining him and running the photographic side of the agency? I didn't want to disappoint him by explaining that my photographs had been taken on one of only three visits to the television studios and that I had never been inside any press agency, so I kept quiet.

By this time my father was fully recovered so both parents could manage without me at the salon, but they advised me against taking such an insecure job. They had a point. Taking a few wedding and children's photographs was one thing and photographing a dozen celebrities was another, but that was still a long way from a full time professional photographer's job. They went on to explain that I was secure now in what would be my own business, and that I could stay in hairdressing forever, whereas this photography business was a leap into the dark . . . and an offer I couldn't refuse.

I arrived in Fleet Street in April 1953 at the agency called 'Bishop's Television News Service'. It was above some shops towards the end of the street, just before the *Daily Express* building. To make the move really complete, I decided that I would leave the parental nest and find a flat of my own. I found the perfect place in a studio flat in Rossmore Court, which was a large block of flats in Park Road, just off Regent's Park. The rent was twelve pounds a week. I was ecstatic. Here I was, 21 years old with a camera and a car and London was all around me.

As I was in charge of the photographic output of the agency, it meant that hardened darkroom men and experienced press photographers were working under me. They were all very good to me after the first shock of my arrival had worn off and my photographs started to come in through the agency.

Tony Collins was an experienced darkroom man who taught me the tricks of the trade and how to handle photographic plates, while Len Trevnor was a very good press photographer who generously showed me the ropes and how to 'snatch' pictures.

Up to now I had only photographed people who had wanted to be photographed, but what if they didn't want their picture taken? Len and I sometimes covered the big law court cases and that meant that we would hide in the street behind the court and wait for the poor unfortunate to creep out of the back exit. Armed with a telephoto lens, I would leap out of a doorway, take the photo and then run like hell. I never really considered that I was invading anybody's privacy. As far as I was concerned, I was only responsible for getting a good and sharp picture. The personal side never entered my mind until we got a very important assignment from the *Sunday Pictorial*. A man called Albert Dimes had just come out of jail, having served time for assaulting a gentleman in the nightclub business called Jack Spot. There was a big party being thrown by the local lads for Albert, celebrating his happy homecoming. The *Sunday Pictorial* had paid someone some money to allow a photographer to join in the festivities, and I was that photographer!

Earlier I had been shown a photo of Albert and I soon spotted him. I got my camera out, prefocused it and slid into a good position. Click! It was a great shot of several men in a huddle, with Albert in the middle. Suddenly a rather large hand gripped my shoulder and turned me around and I found myself staring up into the non-blinking face of a Mike Mazurka lookalike from *The Maltese Falcon*. The only problem was that I was no Humphrey Bogart. He asked what I was doing so I explained the deal with the *Pic*. He knew of no deal but did know that there were people present who did not want to have their photographs taken. By this stage he had picked me up by my jacket and had sat me on the bar. I explained that I was a member of the press. His response was to take my camera which disappeared in his large hand. I quickly took it back, opened it and took out the film which I clutched tightly in my hand. He took the film back and rolled it out on the bar and then jerked his thumb in the direction of the door. No more eloquent request could have been made and I bolted for the safety of the London streets.

Most of the time I concentrated on photographing television programmes and I spent the next two years at the studios of Lime Grove or the BBC studios at Alexandra Palace. For a change I would be sent to a film studio and I remember spending many happy days shooting stills at the Douglas Fairbanks film studios at Elstree.

I loved it all, my little A30 was doing about 30,000 miles per year, and I must have taken thousands of pictures. The agency flourished and by this time we had contracts with all the dailies and the Sunday newspapers. I also had assignments from magazines which I was very proud to work for, such as *Picture Post, Paris Match, London Illustrated News, Stern* and *Life*.

One of the most difficult and challenging assignments I ever had was when I was called into the office of Gordon Mackenzie, the picture editor of the *Sunday Graphic*, a long since defunct Kemsley newspaper, but very popular at the time. Kemsley House was a huge, daunting building on

Grays Inn Road, and I was summoned there on a Thursday afternoon, at the time when all good Sunday newspapers were being 'put to bed' (prepared for printing) for the weekend.

To a photographer a picture editor was God and they didn't come any higher than Gordon Mackenzie. He was friendly to me during our meeting but I had heard that he could be ferocious with a long memory when let down. He took me over to his layout desk. 'See that? That's the front page of this Sunday's *Graphic*.'

I looked down at the page. It had a headline above a very large blank square. I was as blank as the square, so I looked at him.

'Have you heard of Anita Ekberg?' he asked sarcastically.

I, like the rest of the world, had most certainly heard of the lady.

'Good,' he said, and went on to explain that the paper was going to be put to bed by eight o'clock that evening, and that there was a dispatch rider going with me to my appointment with Miss Ekberg. My job was to take a photo that was going to fit into that blank space in front of me. I would take the photographs and then hand them to the rider, who would break all speed limits and the sound barrier if necessary to get the pictures back to Kemsley House in time for the print run.

It was all up to me. I looked at Gordon Mackenzie and then back to the front page that thousands of people would be buying that Sunday. Photographing one of the most beautiful women in the world would surely not be too difficult, but there was a catch.

The editor looked at me closely. 'Listen carefully,' he said, 'she's been here for nearly a week and everybody's shot her.' He paused for effect. 'I don't want any of the agency pictures, this one has got to be ours, this has got to be different or I can't use it.'

'Right,' I said, and off I went in my little A30 to the Grosvenor Hotel, Park Lane, followed closely by the dispatch rider.

Anita Ekberg really was the most beautiful creature that any photographer could have in front of his lens, and she knew her stuff. She had posed for some of the best photographers in the world and now here was Malcolm with his little camera! After an hour I knew I was taking pretty pics but they were a waste of time. All the other photographers in London had taken the same photos. Anita had been photographed running through the park, feeding the ducks, talking to the Beefeaters at the Tower, wearing tight sweaters, low sweaters, evening, day and night wear – everything had een done.

After an hour outside the hotel, she was beginning to wilt and I was coming to terms with the fact that I would never work for that editor and probably the whole Kemsley Group of about eleven newspapers again. We returned to her room and she changed clothes as her assistant ordered some tea and I said that we had finished. Anita was really tired and asked me for a cigarette. She put it in her mouth and leaned over for a light. I shot the picture as she blew the smoke through her pouted lips. That was the last shot and the one that was run on the front page that Sunday – and as far as Gordon Mackenzie was concerned, I was his golden boy – for at least a week, anyway, until the next assignment.

Another national newspaper assignment took me to a tiny, musty BBC Radio theatre in Camden Town where the Goon Show was being recorded.

I was warned beforehand that Peter Sellers, when working with Spike Milligan and Harry Secombe, could be very unpredictable.

And so it proved.

I desperately needed a funny picture, but not one of them would oblige. So with the sort of chutzpa that only a 21-year-old green photographer could have I actually adopted the voice of one of Peter Sellers's most famous characters,

Bluebottle, and shouted across the stage: 'I say, you listen to me, I want to take a funny photo of you foolish fellows.'

They stopped the rehearsals, and dead silence followed.

Peter slowly turned around and in his best Richard III voice, pointed at me with his rolled up script and shouted: 'I see a Bluebottle before me and he fucking well does it better than I do!'

There was no redder faced person in the land than me standing in that studio.

Spike sat on the floor with his head in his hands; he shouted across the stage, 'At last we can get rid of bloody Sellers.' They all turned and stared at me . . . finally they took pity and began to get manic. Harry stuck some Polos up his nostrils, Spike stuck his head under Harry's arm and became 'headless'. Peter stuck his hand up the back of his shirt and began to look like Richard III. I got my pictures.

7 Television

By 1955 I was becoming an old pro. I had spent the best part of three years at the BBC Television studios and was getting to know my way around. The agency was doing well and my photographs were regularly appearing in national newspapers and magazines. Without realising it, I absorbed everything that was going on in the studios; I was a familiar figure hiding under or behind the cameras, taking my shots. At that stage though, I only dreamed about becoming a director.

Later I got to know several producers who also directed their own shows. Brian Tesler was one who was very kind to me and allowed me to photograph his productions. I also got to know Bill Lyon Shaw and Eric Fawcett, who were producers noted for their light entertainment productions. At about that time, I shot a photo feature on a young drama producer called Dennis Vance. At the time I didn't realise how influential he was to become in deciding my future career. As all these men worked mainly from studio G in Lime Grove, it very soon became my second home.

Also at this time I started to regularly cover one of the hottest weekend programmes called *What's My Line?* The programme was presented by one of the BBC's biggest stars, Eamonn Andrews, a young Irishman who would sit at a desk opposite his panel of four celebrities each week. By 1955 television was becoming very big and the events that took place live in the evenings in the studio would often become headline news the following day. My photographs taken during *What's My Line?* were always in demand and I got to know the panelists, Lady Barnett, Barbara Kelly, David Nixon and Gilbert Harding, very well. Eamonn Andrews had a long-running battle with Gilbert Harding and each week there would be some sort of 'incident' that I covered which would make my photographs very saleable.

Over the years Eamonn and I became good friends, but that wasn't the case when we first met. I had arrived to cover my first *What's My Line?* which was being made at the Shepherd's Bush Empire and had just photographed the 'mystery guest' which on that particular night was Petula Clark. She had been hiding in her dressing room before the programme began to avoid being seen by the panel. I wandered over to Eamonn and whispered to him that I had just photographed the mystery guest and that the photographs had gone back to Fleet Street via a dispatch rider. Eamonn's eyes nearly popped out of his head as he pinned me against the wall and gave me a proper rollicking: didn't I know that the mystery guest was not to be seen before the programme? How did I get to see her? Who allowed it? Somebody was going to get fired!

Obviously he was tense before the show, so I promised that I would tell no one about the mystery guest. He then said a very rude word that I remembered using in my Anderson shelter, and I was shocked by the intensity of his feelings. After that outburst I avoided him but at the end of the programme he came up to me and put his arm on my shoulder. I remember flinching back. He had been a boxer and I was convinced he was going to hit me, but all he did was to apologise, and after that trauma we both got along famously. I realised then that the programme and its rules were very real and serious to him; he played it straight, and that was something I was to respect him for throughout our friendship.

Although Eamonn was only ten years older than me he was probably the greatest influence on my personal and pro-

fessional life over the next 35 years. I used to look forward
to our meetings after the programme which always involved
a drink or three, then we would meet up with his wife
Grainne and perhaps have a couple more.

It was towards the end of 1955 that the producer of
What's My Line?, Eric Fawcett, asked if I would join him
and his wife for a drink one evening at his mews house at
the back of Portland Place. He was a photography fanatic
and had always studied my equipment in great detail, so not
unnaturally I thought that he wanted some advice on taking
pictures. This was fine, because I wanted to ask him a favour
too. I had just written a script, complete with camera directions, for a television programme which was based on a
photography course. I wanted his opinion of it. We had our
drink and then he confided in me that he had just signed a
contract with one of the new commercial television companies, to be head of production.

In those days the BBC was paranoid about the new television stations that were due to open up the following year,
and had banned all producers and artists from ever working
for the BBC again should they defect to the 'enemy'. This
meant that Eric was trusting me with a big secret! He was
worried that the new company, ABC TV, would not have
enough young people to train up as cameramen and he wondered if I would be interested in learning. What
extraordinary timing! I gave him my camera script there and
then and confessed that I really wanted to be a television
director, not a cameraman. After all, I argued, I was already
taking pictures and getting very well paid for them.

Eric offered me a compromise. If I joined ABC TV as a
television cameraman, then he would appoint me as a trainee
director after a year. There were snags, of course. The starting salary was about £750 per year, half of what I was
already earning, and if I showed no promise as a television
director, then I would be out of the door in a flash!

So there it was. I could give up my well-established

position at the agency for less than half the salary with no promise that I wouldn't be booted out within one year. Again my parents made an impassioned plea for me to keep my present job and not push my luck with such a crackpot idea. Edward Bishop thought I was raving mad and was not at all pleased. With all that encouragement, I decided to go for it and accepted Eric Fawcett's handshake on our private arrangement for me to become a trainee director.

ABC TV was so new that even the name hadn't been fully registered; the heading on my one-year contract said 'Associated Pathe'. In the first week of January 1956, I reported to the training studio in St John's Wood, a converted chapel with a large wooden floor. It was then that I met the other 50 youngsters who were also trainees, some as cameramen, others as soundmen and many who wanted to be directors. It seemed to me that directing was the one job that they all wanted.

It wasn't until February that year that the company officially became the Associated British Corporation or ABC Television, as it came to be known. Its studios were to be at Elstree and we would be moving in shortly, but meanwhile the training with television cameras and studio equipment was progressing very slowly. There was more to learn than I had anticipated. Then my world began to disintegrate with a series of unplanned setbacks. The first began with a request from the company for all of us to join the television union, the ACTT, otherwise known as the Allied Cinema and Television Technicians union. That was no problem, but the next announcement was a bombshell. Elstree was banned by the union for all television production; it was decreed that only films could be made there! ABC TV had a licence to transmit its programmes only from the North and Midlands and only on weekends, therefore, without Elstree, it would not be making any programmes from London once its studios were ready in Manchester. The upshot was I would have to move up to Manchester or quit. This was not good news, but things could get worse – and they did.

Eric Fawcett had a disagreement with the company, quit his position and somehow persuaded the BBC to take him back. What about my deal to become a trainee director? I took this question to the new head of production. 'What deal?' he asked. Obviously my handshake with Eric had not been legally binding. There ended my first television lesson ... always get it in writing.

There was no going back. I completed my training as a cameraman and moved to Wardour Street in Soho, into a small makeshift studio above some offices. We used this as a temporary site to transmit some programmes for the North and Midlands on Sunday afternoons, enabling the Capitol cinema in Didsbury, Manchester, to be altered into our main television studio.

One of the programmes we transmitted was called *Coffee Time* and was presented by an amiable presenter called Cy Grant, who also played the guitar. His signature tune was called 'Memories Are Made Of This'. It was live, of course, everything was as video tape was still in its experimental stages in the USA.

In this production I was given the dubious honour of being the chief tracker for the senior cameraman, who sat on a six foot long trolley with a camera and seat on a large arm. His name was Ken Jackson and he was a very experienced cameramen from the BBC. My responsibility, however, was to get the camera trolley (it was called a 'pathfinder') to the right place on the studio floor at the right time, which was done by marking the positions with chalk during rehearsals. Unfortunately I had chosen yellow chalk without realising that only scenery was marked in this colour. This created utter confusion with props and scenery scattered across the camera path.

My first transmission was, therefore, a total disaster. Nobody said anything at the time but I was not asked to be a chief tracker ever again.

8 First Stop, Manchester

I bought my first sports car in June 1956. It was a white Triumph TR2 and I was extremely proud of it if not a little terrified of its speed. But there was no speed limit on the new M1 motorway, so off I went to Manchester in top gear.

As I drove up the motorway I thought back on how my life had changed and then reminisced on one of the last photographic jobs I had done during the previous year. I had been covering the BBC's new programme with Eamonn Andrews called *This Is Your Life*. It was an American format that the BBC were not sure would work in the United Kingdom. Ralph Edwards, the American deviser and presenter of the programme in the US, had been persuaded to come over and do the very first show, after which Eamonn was due to take over and do the rest of the nine programmes.

The first guest of the series was to be footballer Stanley Matthews, but a newspaper blew the secret four days before the live show, and as an emergency, Ralph Edwards and BBC producer Leslie Jackson decided to turn the tables on Eamonn and make him the very first subject. When Ralph Edwards said, 'This is your life, Eamonn Andrews', Eamonn was so stunned that all he could think of in reply was, 'Blimey!' I was there to take some very good photographs of his flabbergasted features, which made all the following day's newspapers. The programme became an instant hit and was to become a major part of my life some sixteen years later.

* * *

Money was my immediate problem because the flat in London cost £600 a year rent while my salary was £750. Although continued freelance photographic work in London would get me through, living in Manchester at weekends would make the situation impossible. To solve the problem I joined forces with a fellow cameraman called John Conway and together we found a couple of rooms above a grocery shop in Didsbury, just across from the Manchester studios.

I became a cameraman on outside broadcasts, which was a novel and exciting experience. *Holiday Town Parade*, presented by MacDonald Hobley, was one of the big shows at the time. I knew MacDonald from my BBC days; he was not only a professional but also great fun to work with, and he held wonderful parties after the programme.

Many local people, pleased with the publicity that independent television brought to the Manchester area, began to wine and dine the 'new television boys' and that's when the social scene began to get out of hand. Life became a non-stop party. After each show the booze was free and the atmosphere a heady mixture of excitement coupled with a feeling of doing something new that had never been seen in the country before. It felt as if we could do anything we wanted to! Riotous parties led to hushed-up newspaper stories. On one occasion a local beauty queen woke up after having drunk too much champagne, only to find herself in a hotel bed with an important television executive. The story went that she fell out of the bed and hit her head on the side table, cutting her forehead and drawing some blood. She panicked and ran down the main corridor of the hotel in hysterics – and nothing else.

Within the year, one of the studio administrators had committed suicide, followed by another suicide of a studio technician. There was even a stabbing incident between a producer and his production assistant. By the end of 1956 I had left the television camera and became a studio floor manager.

Things were still so new that within two months I was writing the camera scripts (the script detailing which camera will film which shot from which angle during a show) for the director of the programme I was working on, and when the chance came I directed one of the twenty minute programmes on my own. It felt like jumping into deep water and finding out that I could swim reasonably well. All my past experience with setting up photographic scenes and angles, choosing lenses and shots came to my aid. I could do it!

In 1957 Dennis Vance became head of production at ABC TV and planned to launch the company's first fully networked light entertainment programme series called *Can Do* starring Jon Pertwee. He was looking for a director and remembered me from my photo days at the BBC. Would I direct the new series?

Would I? I accepted on the spot. As I was a relative novice, Dennis agreed to be executive producer to keep an eye on me, but he needn't have worried. Jon Pertwee was a tower of strength and the programme was a resounding success. It consisted of stunts carried out by various celebrities, and money could be won by the contestants providing that they guessed whether the celebrity could do the stunt or not. The prizes went up to £1,500, and the stunts were live.

I remember that we had some truly memorable ones on the show. Once we had a gorgeous model called Sabrina, clad in a bikini, diving into a twenty-foot glass cage full of water in order to find and open an oyster with a pearl inside. We also had an American insert into one programme from Coniston Water where April Olrich, a glamorous singer, attempted to water ski and remove a pair of baggy trousers without falling over. Stanley Baker climbed a rope across a 25-foot 'ravine' and put his back out while Lonnie Donegan nearly came to grief performing a shooting trick. The gun had been loaded with live ammunition by mistake and when he pointed it at his head and pulled the trigger, the .22 rifle should have killed him. Fortunately for Lonnie, the gun jammed!

The programme came from Aston in Birmingham, but my production office was in Wardour Street in London. Every week my production secretary and I would travel to Birmingham and record the show, then return to London the following day to plan next week's programme.

The series was in fact a great success and I was called in to see Howard Thomas, the managing director of ABC Television. He was God as far as I was concerned, and it threw me a little off balance to find him sitting back in his chair with his feet on the edge of his desk.

'Well done,' he said. 'I was against you doing the series at first, because I thought you were far too young, but you did a good job.' He then took his feet from his desk and leaned closer to me. He motioned me to come nearer. 'Just remember one important thing,' he said.

I couldn't wait to hear this revelation. I leaned in and concentrated on what was to come.

'Never split your infinitives.'

I stared back at him in silence for what seemed a very long time.

'Never,' I promised him faithfully, and I meant it.

How could I split something whose identity was a complete mystery to me?

9 Whiter Than White

I n 1957 my contract was renewed – only this time as a director! I had achieved my ambition without Eric Fawcett's help. My salary rocketed to £2,000 a year, but so did my spending. I was still broke. I realised how lucky I was because I was the only one from those St John's Wood trainee days to make it as a director. Yet what was I going to do next?

My series was over and there wasn't anything to follow it at that time, so I was given some commercials to do. All experienced directors would turn down making commercials because they were considered as inferior to programmes, but I was happy to do them. For the next few months I became immersed in an Omo detergent ad which was followed by commercials for Daz, Hoover and Persil.

All of these were very big market brands and I came into contact with the biggest of the advertising agencies such as J. Walter Thompson, Mather and Crowther and Procter and Gamble. At the time ABC Television experienced a slump in finances and some drama, feature and sports directors were laid off, but nobody interfered with me. I was the only director at the time who was actually making money for the company. Along with the slump came an added importance on making commercials, as it was the advertisers who were injecting money into the company, and of course, I had worked with the major ones.

Commercials were in a world of their own. My most

memorable one was one I did for Armitage Budgerigar Seed. It was very straightforward, with the presenter picking up a packet of seed and then the camera would pan to a beautiful cage with an even more beautiful budgie singing inside.

An hour before this commercial was due to be shot the studio had been used for a special dance rehearsal which involved smoke effects swirling around the dancers. We entered the studio and did all our rehearsals without the little bird, which was to be placed in position at the very last second because this was a live transmission and we didn't want his singing to interfere with the presenter's speech. The studio air seemed clear and smokeless enough to us but obviously not clear enough for our budgie, who – when the camera panned to him on transmission – was lying very dead at the bottom of his cage.

Armitage did get some fantastic publicity in the papers the next day, but were not over impressed by our methods.

The new year of 1958 dawned, and the slump was still with us; by this stage even my commercials were being cancelled and I hoped ABC and I would survive to see the end of the year. Then my father had another mild heart scare and I thought it was time to make some decisions concerning the family. I took a two month leave of absence and negotiated the sale of 'Maison Morris' together with my parents' flat in the Caledonian Road. When that was completed I arranged their retirement in Brighton, where hopefully my father could fully recover.

When I returned to ABC I found that there was now a new controller of programmes called Ronald Rowson. We did not get along from the time when I wrote him a memo which I did not have time to sign and asked my secretary to sign on my behalf. I was called in to his office and was given a sharp dressing down. He was furious that I had sent him a note and not signed it. The poor state of the television industry and his programme schedules did not apparently upset him as much as my missing signature. I explained the circumstances, but to no effect, and it became clear to me that from then on I was going to be swimming against the tide. The man was my boss and he didn't like me. I sat in a small coffee bar in Soho that evening and wondered whether I should have sold 'Maison Morris' so hastily.

Several months earlier the local advertising sales manager of ABC had left Manchester and had gone to Newcastle-upon-Tyne, to help put Tyne Tees Television on the air. His name was Walter Williamson, an ex-RAF navigator with a DFC from the war and a wonderful Yorkshireman to boot. I had spent many hours with Walter and his wonderful wife, Edith, over a drink or two in the Parrswood pub opposite the studios in Manchester, and we had become good friends. A week after my pasting, I heard from Walter who said that Tyne Tees was a wonderful company being run by a programme controller who knew me very well. His name was Bill Lyon Shaw and he was one of the BBC producers I had photographed many times back in the Lime Grove days. Much more important was the fact that he was looking for a young, experienced director. I was on the phone to Bill Lyon Shaw instantly.

I arranged to meet Bill again together with the owners of the company, George and Alfred Black. I was given a very warm reception. George and Alfred were the sons of the famous theatrical impresario Alfred Black whose theatres were an important part of the London showbusiness scene. Nearly every big star had worked for their father at one time or another. 'Mr Alfred' and 'Mr George' were carrying on the family tradition with theatres and cinemas all over the country. Tyne Tees Television was their new baby and they wanted to handpick all the directors and producers themselves to ensure that they were getting the best. They were the first to admit that they knew precious little about television, so that was why they asked Bill Lyon Shaw to be controller of programming.

It was the August Bank Holiday in 1959 when I loaded

the last of my London home, right down to the teapot and record player, into my new VW Beetle. As Tyne Tees Television was on air seven days a week, I couldn't get away with just commuting up at weekends. I pointed my Beetle towards the north and off I drove.

It was just over five hours later that I drove across Newcastle's famous suspension bridge and turned right down City Road to the studios. The first thing I noticed was that the studios were opposite Procter and Gamble's main office – well, at least I knew they liked my commercials! I went straight into the Tyne Tees Television studio reception, only to find that the studios were closed! It was a Bank Holiday, and as video tape had been around now for a little while, all the local programmes had been pre-recorded.

Walter Williamson had advised me that good accommodation in Newcastle was hard to find and that I had better find 'digs' or a cheap hotel for a while and look for a flat later. Then again, I had always ignored good advice, and checking my AA road map, drove ten miles to Tynemouth in search of a flat. It was now almost four o'clock, and I only had a few hours before it got dark.

One hour later I was the resident of a one bedroomed flat at the top of a large Victorian house right on the seafront. I had a wonderful view of the seafront and local lifeboat station. I looked out across the sandy beach and felt rather pleased with myself. It had been a hot day and a sticky drive so I did not unpack the car. I found my suitcase and pulled out a swimsuit, but I did not anticipate my legs turning blue as I ran into the freezing cold sea. Then I realised just how far north I was!

I was to live in Newcastle for the next five years, doing the hardest work I had ever known.

Those years were without doubt the happiest of my life.

10 Geordie Land

T
yne Tees Television was a true regional company in that a large part of its transmission came from the ITV network, but the rest were local programmes, made to please itself. And please itself and its audience it certainly did.

George and Alfred Black were showbusiness people, and so was Bill Lyon Shaw, so it was only natural that the programme emphasis was on light entertainment. All the young directors were chosen with this in mind. Many of my young friends at the time went on to bigger and better things. David Croft went on to write, produce and direct, *Are You Being Served?*, *Hi de Hi*, *'Allo, 'Allo* and *You Rang, M'Lord?*, while Philip Jones went on to produce and direct *Thank Your Lucky Stars*, *Big Night Out*, the Bruce Forsyth specials, *The Sinatra Concert* and many others. He was to become the controller of light entertainment for Thames Television. Another friend, Keith Beckett, was an ex-ballet dancer who later became one of the top freelance director/producers, with *The Benny Hill Show*, the Tom Jones specials, and the *Tommy Steel Special* to his credit. Another colleague, Austin Mitchell, went on to become an MP, while the name of our young station announcer was David Hamilton. There was also a very pretty young announcer called Valerie Pitts, who was later to become Lady George Solti.

All of us were shown the ropes by Bill Lyon Shaw, and we were all greatly influenced by the theatrical atmosphere created by George and Alfred Black. The programmes were hard work but great fun to work on. I was involved with the daily hour long *One O'clock Show*, the children's programmes, the music specials and also the features and documentaries. If all this sounds frantic it's because it was. Sometimes I would also direct some commercials as well. Tyne Tees was one of the biggest regional companies and was very proud of its output.

All major artists would appear on Tyne Tees through their association with either George and Alfred Black, Bill Lyon Shaw, or his assistant controller, Peter Glover. Peter was an ex-dancer and had directed a very successful series for ATV in London called *Cool for Cats* which had featured a young new dancer called Una Stubbs. When he came to Tyne Tees he had just finished working with a young chorus girl called Audrey Hepburn.

We were lucky enough to attract all the big stars – Alma Cogan, Bruce Forsyth, Norman Wisdom, Howard Keel, Brenda Lee, Norman Vaughan, Dick Haynes, Spike Milligan, Harry Secombe, Des O'Connor and Tony Hancock all made appearances on Tyne Tees Television. There were also the wonderful 'resident' artists who lived in the area, such as Terry and Peggy O'Neil and Jack Haigh, who were the stars of the *One O'clock Show* and were dearly loved by the north-east audience. There was a special bond between these artists and the directors because we all depended on each other, week after week.

One of the performers I got to know well around this time was Des O'Connor. He was developing his own act which was very wide ranging indeed. He did a standup routine which was packed with fast and funny jokes but he also liked acting in sketches. This was hugely interesting for a young television director developing his own technical tricks, and we became instant pals, going on to have great laughs over the years in many variety shows.

In those days Des lived near Reigate and was a dab hand

at DIY, having rebuilt his own kitchen. His wife Gill was lovely and they had two angelic daughters, Tracy and Samantha, who were about six and eight at the time. Des was booked for a summer season at Blackpool and I happily accepted his invitation to join them on their drive to the Golden Mile. I was in a particularly good mood because it promised to be a few weeks of fun and laughs, and also, I had just splashed out and bought a very expensive blazer, trousers and shirt from Simpsons of Piccadilly. We were having a good time except Tracy – or was it Samantha? – who was snuggled half across my lap. Shyly she looked up at me and gave me a very cute smile. Then she managed to empty her entire stomach contents over me. I instantly became a sitting sick bag, and although the whole family sympathised, Des had tears of laughter pouring down his face watching me change by the roadside.

Those tears kept erupting all the way to Blackpool.

It took some years before I got my revenge when a very enthusiastic relative of mine, autograph hunting, knocked a glass of wine over Des's cream trousers.

It was the best laugh I had at my wedding party.

Whatever work was going, I was doing it. In this way I gained priceless experience that was to sustain me for the rest of my career. I even had the chance to work on my first situation comedy which I co-wrote with a young freelance writer called Brad Ashton. It featured an unknown comic called Derek Dene, whose style was somewhere between Norman Wisdom and Charlie Drake. He had the right sort of sympathetic approach which made him the perfect lovable failure in whatever he did, and we were also very lucky to get the well known comedy actor Sydney Tafler to appear on the series, which in the end ran for over ten weeks. The sitcom featured yet another comedian with a very strange sense of humour called Bob Todd. He later became one of the regular TV players with Benny Hill.

I was also fortunate enough to make some documentaries

abroad. My favourite was called *The Multi-Million Promise* and dealt with the last voyage of the *Queen Elizabeth* to New York. Cunard had really laid out the red carpet and gave me a first class state room for the trip. I was surrounded by luxury: walnut panels and antique furniture, brass fittings, thick carpets and a king-sized four-poster bed on a raised dais. It was the most marvellous experience. Six days later we were in New York and then flew back to get the programme on air by that weekend.

Back at Tyne Tees I was given a new project, a series that would appeal especially to teenagers. The programme was called *Young at Heart* and it would have the latest pop music on the show, along with a feature film and a live group performing their songs with some youngsters dancing along in the audience.

The format was no problem, but finding the right presenter was. If we chose an experienced artist he would probably be too old, but if we chose a youngster, he would not have the experience to do the job. This was going to be a difficult one to solve, but one day Peter Glover asked me to try someone out. The man he had his eye on was the successful manager of the Glasgow Mecca Dance Hall. This young man turned up on the day of his interview dressed in a silver lamé jacket with long silver shoes that were turned up at the ends. To finish the effect off, he was smoking a huge and expensive Monte Cristo cigar and his hair was pink. I asked him what his name was.

'It's funny that you should ask,' he said. I couldn't see why it was funny, and tried not to stare at his hair. 'I'm Jimmy Savile, who are you?'

He did the first pilot show and he was great. To this day I don't know how he did it, because he had never been in a television studio before, but he was just great! He kept repeating the words, 'How's about that then?', which started to drive me mad, but his sheer sense of fun and true enjoyment was infectious. After the show I introduced him to Mr George and Mr Alfred, who were a little taken aback.

After Jimmy had left their office, they asked me if I was serious about him doing the show. I said I was.

'He'll never get anywhere,' said George Black.

I asked them to come over to the window and have a look at the street below. They were puzzled but came over and looked down at the beautiful new white Rolls Royce parked below.

'Whose car is that?' they asked.

'That car belongs to the fellow you have just said will not make it!'

Young at Heart was a great success, and we all know what happened to the Mecca manager from Glasgow!

By 1964 I had moved several times from Tynemouth to Whitley Bay and then into Jesmond, the 'trendy' part of Newcastle. I had many good friends there and I would have been happy to stay forever, but then came an offer from London that I could not refuse.

11 Live From London

I answered the ringing telephone. It was from ABC Television. 'Eamonn Andrews is leaving the BBC because they have dropped *This Is Your Life* and he's joining ABC Television. Do you want to produce his new late night series?'

I drove south across the Newcastle suspension bridge with mixed emotions. I was excited at the prospect of being able to work with Eamonn on what would be a very important programme for him, ABC and me, but I was also leaving some very good friends, and Newcastle had become my home.

I had driven up in a VW Beetle and was returning in a Jaguar XK 150, but that wasn't the only change. I was now very much more experienced and confident in my work and judgement.

The series was due to start on Sunday nights from September 1964. I rejoined ABC TV six months earlier, in February. I had been away for five years. I was now 32 and I had survived eight years in television. ABC's new programme controller was Brian Tesler, the young producer who had, back in my Fleet Street days, been so kind in allowing me to photograph his productions live. ABC had put together a very large team for the new series and the executive producer was Lloyd Shirley. Lloyd was Canadian and he and I had worked together a long time ago and got on very well. As I was mainly producing on this series, I was given a new young director straight from the camera department called Tom Clegg. Tom went on to become a first class director and directed many episodes of *The Sweeney*. There was also a production assistant for the director, a programme secretary for me as well as four programme researchers.

The programme was going to be a late night talk show and would deal with a wide range of topics, from showbusiness to politics and anything else in between, and there was also one music spot in the middle of the programme to break up the talk. Although these days this format is a very familiar type of programme, back in 1964 the concept only existed in America. Our team were all going into unknown production territory and because of the wide range of topics open for discussion, it was considered wise to bring in an adviser so Tony Jay, a freelance features producer, joined us for our weekly meetings at our Hanover Square offices.

We only had four months to go to the first transmission date, and still the series did not have a name. I suggested that we should call it *The Eamonn Andrews Show* but this was rejected by Eamonn, who had made a programme by that name some years earlier for the BBC where the producer had persuaded Eamonn to sing on the programme.

The singing spot was a disaster and Eamonn had hated the title ever since.

Brian Tesler wanted to call it *The Sunday Night Show*, but then I dropped my bombshell. 'I also want to do it live, and to say to the audience that it's live.' Eamonn liked the idea but Brian was shaking his head.

'People don't care whether it's live or not,' he said, 'and anyway, it's too dangerous. You can't be sure as to what anyone will say.'

'Exactly my point,' I agreed, warming to my subject. 'It's dangerous, so let's tell the audience that, by an announcement before the titles go up on the screen. Let's say: "LIVE FROM LONDON".'

I won and for the next few years, John Benson's marvellous voice was heard each week at 10.30 on Sunday nights across the country: 'Live from London, The Eamonn Andrews Show!'

After a year Lloyd Shirley went on to other projects and I was left to run the show, together with its two writers, Tom Brennand and Roy Bottomley. We were a powerful little team, which tried to make the best programme possible. We would sit in Eamonn's small office in a wing of his Chiswick home by the river, and debate and argue on the merits of the four guests, who they should be and what the running order should be.

The programme was a big success with good ratings, the first programme, in fact, which went out after 10.30 at night to make it into television's top twenty ratings. The audience at home loved it but the press didn't, and Eamonn took a beating in the papers week after week – but the ratings got higher and higher.

The ratings probably rose because Eamonn allowed various comedians to tell a 'risqué' joke or story on the show. I remember one programme in particular when we invited a young New York nightclub comedian to appear. It was his first English television appearance and neither Eamonn nor the audience knew who the hell he was. His name was Woody Allen.

Woody Allen was one of the most nervous people I had ever met.

He had never been to London before and his hand shook when we met, while his face was that of someone who was about to encounter some terrible torture and his apprehensive look was topped by thin wispy red hair. He had a couple of attractive girls with him who were constantly reassuring him that everything was OK.

Some days before his first appearance on the show I met him at the bar of the Playboy Club in London's Park Lane. We talked about the programme and he told me that he had a rule that he did not compete with other comedians, so would I not book any more for the show on which he was due to appear. I agreed, but a day before the programme went out a special story broke about Spike Milligan and since the live programme tried to be as topical as possible I booked him for that night.

I asked Spike not to muck around with Woody and he said he would not.

Woody, on the other hand, was furious; he was terrified of Spike who had, as always, the audience in the palm of his hand. Spike, however, was as good as his word and made no interruptions while Woody was talking. After the show Woody complained and I told him that Spike was not a comedian in the sense of telling stand-up jokes and that the programme had been a very big success for Woody. Only when his two girls came over and told him just how good he was did Woody relax, which in his case means down to only moderate shaking.

Only recently I had a letter from him asking me for a copy of that programme as his copy had been wiped by a busy company accountant.

I do hope that 30 years on, Woody is not still worrying about that night. In fact, he was brilliant.

He started by greeting Eamonn live on air and telling him that he was celebrating an anniversary that very night.

'Oh,' said Eamonn innocently. 'A birthday?'

'No,' said Woody, 'it's a year today since my wife slashed her wrists!'

There was a stunned silence and Eamonn, a staunch Catholic and Papal Knight, took in what had just been said. Eamonn swallowed and forced a laugh while Woody ploughed on. 'My Jewish family in New York had a Rabbi who was very liberal.'

'Oh,' said Eamonn, wondering what he was in for.

'Yes, very liberal, he was a Nazi.'

That got a very big laugh and from then on Woody

warmed to the audience and told them that his ex-wife was so immature that she interrupted him in his bath in order to sink his boats.

Woody came back on the programme many more times after that traumatic first night.

Very soon Tom, Roy and I began to realise that here was a potentially powerful situation to exploit on the programme. How would Eamonn react to . . . whoever? Would someone else tell a terrible joke? Would someone say a rude word? The suspense was unmissable and the audience figures just grew and grew.

The actor Laurence Harvey telephoned me from Los Angeles to ask whether he could tell a risqué camel joke on the show. Sitting opposite Eamonn on the night, Laurence talked about the lost foreign legionnaires, who on hearing that some new camels had arrived at the post, all rushed out to see them.

'Why is everybody rushing?' said the new recruit.

'Do you want an ugly one?' replied the sergeant.

Most people the following day were repeating the joke and the press decided that this was the 'public crucifixion' of Eamonn Andrews. Even Howard Thomas, the managing director, came into my office the morning after the show and asked why I had allowed the camel joke to be told.

'I don't see how you can have a sexual innuendo about a camel; it's all in the mind,' I said, looking as blank as I could.

Howard Thomas started to say something then stopped. He was not convinced or amused.

The programme continued to attract some of the biggest names in the world: Michael Caine, Richard Harris, Randolph Churchill, A. J. P. Taylor, Tony Hancock, Zsa Zsa Gabor, Charlton Heston, George Raft, Lauren Bacall, S. J. Perelman, J. B. Priestley, Shirley Bassey, Tony Bennett, James Garner and many more appeared during the four years that I produced the programme. I have some special memories of those magical years which just must go on record.

Jane Fonda was booked for the programme and, being a great fan of hers, I agreed to pick her up from the airport on the Friday before the Sunday show. I drove her to the Savoy and I gave her my home telephone number in case she had any problems before the show on Sunday. Now by this time I had met the great love of my life, except things were not progressing quite as I would have wished. Nevertheless, on the Saturday evening before the programme I was entertaining the lady in question at my Chiswick flat. The mood was somehow stilted until the telephone rang as I was making coffee. I asked my guest to take the call and was surprised by the hushed tones in which I was informed that it was Jane Fonda for me. Jane simply wanted me to sort something mundane out, but my guest was so overwhelmed by the prospect that my 'other woman' was Jane Fonda that the evening took off in a new and more attractive direction!

I never did thank Jane Fonda for helping me and my wonderful romance, so I formally do so now.

It's amazing how sometimes very big stars go against what you expect.

Bob Hope had agreed to do the show providing that we would meet him before the programme to go over the best possible stories he could give us. He is a perfectionist and wanted to be sure that the English audience would understand and appreciate the particular stories he would use, so Tom, Roy and I went along one evening to the Grosvenor Hotel and Bob Hope gave us his 'audition'. He tried out every story he had for the programme and gave us an hour's performance. He was just brilliant and we were in stitches.

By coincidence, Bing Crosby was also in London at the same time and agreed to surprise Bob Hope by throwing a golf ball onto the stage at the end of Bob's spot. He didn't have any clubs with him so I lent him my very tatty golf bag which he threw over his shoulder as he walked on. He was wonderful and the show that week was an absolute smash.

After the programme Bing said he had to leave early and would I arrange for a car to take him from the Teddington studios back to town. I went down to the side entrance to wait with him until the car arrived. I couldn't believe I was standing outside in the nippy Teddington air with one of my all-time idols, talking with him about those wonderful *Road* movies. I felt I was in seventh heaven.

Roy Bottomley contributed more ideas to the programme than anyone else and it was Roy who spotted the *Esquire* picture spread of the then-unknown Raquel Welch who was about nineteen years old and quite stunning.

Why not invite this girl on to the programme, he suggested. Why not indeed? thought I.

Raquel was staying in London for a promotional visit organised by her husband, who was also acting as her press agent. He knew the promotional value of our programme and agreed that Raquel would wear something special for the occasion.

She did; she came on the programme wearing a very short, skin-tight gold lamé dress that was sensational!

I don't know to this day if she was wearing a body stocking underneath that dress, but the lighting on our show made it look transparent and there was no doubt in my mind as to what conversations were about all over the country on the following Monday morning!

The Beatles were booked to appear on the programme when they arrived back from their sensational first trip to America. 'Beatlemania' was at its height and their manager Brian Epstein advised me to make special arrangements for all our protection. I thought this was a little dramatic but I laid on double the normal security men around our Teddington studios. The Beatles arrived and I took them for some lunch in our reserved riverside room. While we were lunching, the security was holding up well even though a huge crowd of screaming girls was pressing against the studio gates. Suddenly a young girl walked into the dining room. She had taken a small boat along the river and climbed up the bank, dodging the guards by coming through the back of the studio grounds. She had only taken two steps when three security men pounced on her and she was being bundled out of the room when Paul got up and stopped them. He went to the girl who went into a complete trance. He wrote his name on the back of a sheet of script and gave it to her and he then put his arm around her as she was led out. The crowd saw the girl and another shriek went up.

It was all a bit scary but the boys had become used to it and I noticed that John Lennon had not paused in eating his meal throughout the whole incident.

His eggs, beans, tomatoes and toast had all vanished.

After the meal John took me to one side and said that they would be singing live. I instantly panicked as Brian Epstein had told me that they were going to mime to their latest record, which meant that I had not booked any sound facilities to cover the song. I rushed out to find some sound men at short notice, and found that the entire studio was surrounded by thousands of young girls. They were all pushing against the gates of the studio, while some were attempting to climb the fifteen foot high wire fence behind our dining room. I began to sweat because I couldn't find the sound men and went back to explain to Paul, who was their spokesman. He looked surprised and said that it was not necessary because they would be miming. I looked at John, who without looking up said, 'Y'eah, that's what I understood.' I'd been had by the mischievous John Lennon, who continued to make me nervous for the rest of the day. In the end extra police had to be called in to handle the crowd and I was very pleased when the programme was over and the Fab Four went on their way.

* * *

One of the programme's greatest coups was to get Lucille Ball to make an appearance. I was amazed and awestruck when it was arranged for her to have a meeting with me at our Hanover Square offices in London's West End to set up the details.

On the day, I made sure that my office was cleaned, tidied and 'dressed' with a wall chart and flowers, coffee tables, extra filing cabinets and anything that would project the image of a dynamic television producer doing the world's best talk show.

They were right on time at 12.00 midday.

I greeted them in my best business suit with a suitable handkerchief casually exposed from my jacket pocket at just the right level. It should have been just right because it had taken me a great deal of time getting it that casual.

The meeting began, coffee and drinks were rejected and so I began my carefully rehearsed description of the programme. I didn't get very far because although two of my telephones had been taken over by my PA to avoid incoming calls, the third phone was a direct outside line and it rang.

The telephone call was from my mother reminding me that I was due to visit them that evening for dinner. This was not the stuff of world executives; it was my worst nightmare but I could still save the situation by getting a goodbye in before she got underway.

I quickly put my hand over the receiver. 'So sorry,' I said across my tidy desk to Lucille, 'it's a filming schedule, won't take a moment.'

'Good to hear from you,' I said, in my best filmlike manner down the phone.

'So are you coming here at last?' Mother said.

I had to keep it businesslike. 'The answer to your question is yes, our appointment is still on, I shall look forward to it. Must go now because I'm in the middle of a meeting.' I smiled at everyone.

'You've got an appointment?' she said. 'Oh your father

will be upset. LEW –' She was now shouting across the phone to my father – 'Lew, he's not coming.'

I drew a deep breath. 'Yes, I shall definitely be there. Thank you so much.'

'Oh good. Lew, he's changed his mind, now he's coming.'

As the nightmare continued I looked across at one of the world's biggest legends and quickly said, 'Thank you, good-bye.'

Not quick enough. 'So what do you want to eat?'

I was getting quite sweaty now. 'Oh, I think the same as last time, it all went so well.'

'It went well? So what can go wrong with chicken?'

I began to avoid eye contact with Lucille's manager.

'My point exactly.'

'So you want chicken?'

'Yes.'

'With soup?'

'Yes.'

'We had chicken yesterday.'

This was now serious. I put my hand over the phone once again. 'I'm terribly sorry, this is a film shoot and it's someone who's going abroad the day after.'

I continued grimly. 'I understand we did that before. Why don't you make your own forecast?'

'Forecast? All I want to know is what you want to eat.'

I didn't answer. 'Are you there? What about a nice piece of fish?'

I reached for the nearest file and looked inside. 'Now that's perfect. Goodbye.'

'Fried or boiled? No, wait a minute, your father doesn't want fish.'

I opened my mouth to speak, but it was too late. Living away from home, I had lost my timing.

'We're having chicken; boiled or roast? If you have it boiled I can also do a nice soup with knadels.'

'Thank you, that's the deal.' I slammed down the phone

and much to my guests' surprise, gently pulled the telephone wire from its socket.

I had to wipe my forehead because the sweat was running down into my eyes and the salt began to sting.

We finished the meeting and all was well.

More than ten years later, Ralph Edwards, the deviser of *This Is Your Life*, took me to Chasens, a famous Hollywood restaurant. Dining nearby was Lucille Ball. I went over and confessed all.

Lucille had a very fruity laugh and she laughed so much that when she finished she wrote some notes on the back of her menu and asked me whether I would mind if she wrote that exchange into a special *I Love Lucy* show.

My mother is no longer here, but I like to think that perhaps a little of her is still being syndicated around the world.

When Diana Rigg stepped out of *The Avengers*, a massive nationwide publicity campaign followed to find her replacement. When Linda Thorsen was chosen she was immediately invited on to the show. It was her first exposure to the public and a great scoop for the programme.

Linda was very young, sexy with a great figure and she was also intelligent with a fast wit. The programme was very successful for her; she felt she had been well and truly launched. As the producer it was my duty to look after my guests and I was never one to shirk my duty. After the show came a very long session of hospitality where everybody drank loads and then I ordered a studio car to take Linda home. I did not want to drive and since the car was going in the direction of my flat in Chiswick Village I decided to join her. Out of politeness I invited the lady in for a drink, not thinking for one moment that she would accept. She was, however, on a television high, so she accepted. She really was a fabulous dancer and that's what we did for a long time. This is not a bad way to finish an evening I thought, so we decided on one more bottle of champagne to toast her success.

It had been a very long day and I had had a few more drinks than Linda. I sat down, looking at her, and closed my eyes for one second to savour the situation. When I opened them it was one hour later and my new avenger had escaped just as efficiently as she was to do during her adventures with Patrick McNee.

This story still brings tears to my eyes.

In 1966 Tony Hancock agreed to appear on the show. This was a great scoop because he did not appear on television as himself and usually avoided any interviews. I met him at the studios and he was charming, funny and warm. I took him to our 'green room' and we sat and talked about the programme. He would be meeting Eamonn soon and as we talked he became more and more nervous. The programme went out live at 10.30 that evening so he knew that he couldn't take a drink or he would have become a wreck.

After five bitter lemons and three trips to the lavatory he decided to ring his wife Freddie, whom he had banned from coming with him. He asked her in a loud voice why the hell she had let him agree to come on the damn show; it was going to be a disaster. They spoke for nearly 45 minutes before he calmed down and then it was time for the programme. By this stage I was very nervous and told Eamonn to be very careful with Tony on the programme. 'What do you mean "very careful"?' Eamonn asked.

I explained that Tony was almost hyperventilating and that he should be prepared for anything that might happen.

'Wonderful,' said Eamonn and went out to greet the cameras and the audience.

Tony was funny, confident and quite brilliant, the audience loved him and he was very well received. I greeted him after the show with my congratulations, but unsmiling, he rushed past me to the telephone. An hour later, after speaking to his wife, he was phoning his friends, pleading with them to tell him the truth about his live performance.

He and I were both wrecks by the time he left the studio. That was a show that had gone extremely well and I dreaded to think what happened to him when things went badly. He was one brilliant and tormented man.

Eric Morcambe and Ernie Wise had always avoided the programme because they were uneasy in an uncontrolled situation. Nevertheless I was determined to get them on. I was sure that if only I could meet them I could talk them into it.

They were making a film at Pinewood and with the help of some friends I was fixed up to take them both to lunch at the exclusive Pinewood Club. I knew they were consummate professionals and if I could convince them of my and the programme's efficiency, then they would relax and feel safe – and appear live.

I was meeting them at about midday and, of course, the table was booked in my name. I had one programming meeting at Teddington and then I was into my car. I was almost late because I couldn't find the studios, but I made it on time – just.

Eric and Ernie arrived and seemed completely engrossed in their own conversation. We sat down at the table and they began to talk to each other as if I was not there. Eric looked around him and after he was satisfied, he looked at Ernie. 'He's from that programme with Andrews Liver Salts.'

Ernie nodded gravely. 'What does he want?'

I sat opposite them, feeling totally lost.

They went on and on, building a complete act for many minutes, making each other laugh. I had never seen two people so in tune with each other before.

After their last long laugh they paused and I dived in. 'Come on the programme,' I said, very much to the point.

Eric looked at me. 'Thank you. I'll have the chicken salad.'

Ernie said, 'It's fish for me, I'll have the Dover sole.'

'Wow,' said Eric, 'that's very expensive.'

Ernie looked at me deeply. 'He can afford it.'

And so it went on until we finished the lunch. 'Must go,' they said as one.

I got the bill and reached into my jacket pocket. There was nothing there. In my rush I had forgotten to transfer my credit cards and cash into my posh jacket. I had taken two of the top men in the world of entertainment to lunch at the expensive and exclusive Pinewood Club restaurant, and I was a pauper. I looked at them finishing their coffee as I searched again through all my pockets, realising that I did not have anything on me, no cash, no cheques, no credit cards and no identification.

Eric spotted it first. He paused with his cup halfway to his face.

'Ern,' he said in a loud stage whisper, 'Ern . . . he hasn't any mullie.'

Ernie looked at me closely with a deadpan expression.

'You're right, he's skint.'

Eric looked at me with great sympathy. 'They don't like that here, you know.' Eric went on warming to his subject and I could feel another sketch coming on. He drew in his breath with a loud hiss. 'You, kind sir, are in deep, deep trouble.'

The waiter arrived and they both looked at him with secret smiles. They were really enjoying themselves.

'He's got no money,' said Eric. 'He can't pay,' said Ernie.

The waiter looked at them and then at me. I was very red by this time.

'I've left all my money in another suit.' It sounded pathetic.

Eric motioned the waiter to bend over closer to him and then he whispered in a stage voice: 'He produces the Eamonn Andrews show, he doesn't get paid very much.'

I pressed on. 'Can I sign the bill?' They both collapsed back in their chairs and looked at each other.

'Do you remember the last chap who tried to sign for the bill?' Eric looked at Ernie.

'No I don't,' said Ernie.

Eric moved closer and then held Ernie's head between his hands. 'Of course you don't remember.' He looked around him.

Eric then continued in a low voice, 'They don't talk about it any more ... it was terrible, terrible, Ern, it's all been hushed up now.'

They never did come on the show but I did give them a very funny lunch.

Years later I worked with Ernie and Doreen Wise, and I like to regard them today as my good friends. But I shall not forget my lunch with Eric and Ern for a very long time.

There was one programme that without a doubt in my mind will stand out as the most exciting of the entire series. Cassius Clay, or Muhammad Ali as he was then, was fighting Henry Cooper in a World Championship fight in London on the Saturday before our show. We did all the deals we could with the promoter Jarvis Astaire, who thought, quite correctly, that if Muhammad Ali won the fight (which he did), our programme would be the perfect way of correcting his 'bad boy' image.

Then suddenly another booking that we had been pursuing for a year came to us. Noel Coward was in London that week and would do the programme. We were still not finished. We also had Dudley Moore and to top it all, a world famous Hollywood star had also agreed to come on the show that week. Our show's guests for that week were Muhammad Ali, Noel Coward, Dudley Moore and Lucille Ball. It was the peak of the series. After the show I remember thanking Noel Coward for his kindness to me when I had photographed him on the *Night of a Hundred Stars* at the Palladium back in 1952.

Brian Tesler had warned me about the programme being live and his warning became valid in the third year. It started with a small but frightening incident during a programme in mid-transmission. Eamonn was about to introduce his next guest and looked down at his notes. When he looked up a tall young man just walked on and stood beside him. Eamonn knew instantly that he was not part of the show – and so did I in the control room – but at that moment there was nothing I could do. Eamonn looked at him and without hesitation said that he did not know who he was or what he wanted, but he was welcome to come and sit down. The stranger was so startled at this invitation that he sat quietly at the end of a settee.

Our second incident wasn't so dramatic but proved to be more expensive. Clement Freud was a very witty newspaper columnist who was always welcome on the programme. On one particular week he was debating the possible joys of eating out. He casually mentioned that he had eaten out that week at a well-known restaurant, which he named, but then complained that he had not been happy with his fish dinner. A small red light blinked in the back of my mind which I ignored until later in the week when ABC's company lawyers got in touch with me. The restaurant Clement had named was suing us for libel.

In the end we settled out of court for £5,000, which would not have caused too much trouble but for the next libel suit which came a few weeks later.

Arthur Dooley was a passionate sculptor from Liverpool, a city he loved dearly. His complaint was with its most recent architecture and he named a company which he said built terrible buildings, calling them 'gangsters'. That resulted in another £5,000 settlement out of court and the end of our 'Live from London' days.

The announcement was now 'From London, The Eamonn Andrews Show' and we prayed that people would not notice that we had dropped the 'Live'. The programme, through some technical magic, was now going on to one video tape machine and was then being played back straightaway on another, and this had the effect of delaying the transmission by five seconds, which in theory would give me time to cut out the sound, or 'bleep' it. This was agreed after a strong request came down from the board of directors of the company.

The first person to get this treatment was Michael Crawford, who told a really harmless story of a girl who was driving a sports car. He went on to describe her as 'the sort of snooty girl who looks as if she has a packet of frozen peas between her legs'.

I bleeped 'packet of frozen peas', which had the whole country wondering as to just what it was that the girl had between her legs.

A year later I felt that I had spent enough time on *Live from London* and I handed the programme over to a dapper, cigar-smoking, well regarded producer called Gordon Reece, who did a good job and went on to become a television adviser to Mrs Thatcher some years later.

My old friend Philip Jones was now the controller of the Light Entertainment department and he was happy to give me a new situation comedy called *Gentleman Jim*, which had the most wonderful cast. It starred Jimmy Edwards, Richard Wattis, Pat Coombs and Clive Dunn. The programme went very well and after its run had finished I went on to produce and direct another situation comedy with the wonderful veteran actor Robert Coote, who was a delight to work with. The programme was called *The Best of Enemies* and was set in the House of Commons between a young socialist and a crusty old conservative. It was very successful and was developed into a series which was not produced by me because the year was 1968, and I had another one of my special phone calls.

12 Voulez-vous Habiter en Newcastle?

his time the call was from Tony Jelly, the managing director of Tyne Tees Television. I knew him from my days with the company five years earlier and I wondered why he was ringing me now. 'How would you . . .' – I held my breath – 'like to play golf this weekend at Gleneagles?' My golf had never been that good, but the thought of going to that Scottish shrine of golf was irresistible!

I was also sure that Tony Jelly had something else in mind, well outside the challenges of the game. Towards the end of the weekend we were sitting over a very acceptable dinner in the dining room at Gleneagles. I had been given a vintage double brandy and was smoking a very nice Monte Cristo No. 7.

I waited. 'How would you like the job of programme controller for Tyne Tees Television?' he said. A Programme Controller in television terms is like being God. They are the people who decide what programmes are made, who makes them, what time they will be transmitted and on what day. They are responsible for all the money the company spends on programmes and are accountable only to the managing director and chairman of the company.

At 36, I would be the youngest person ever to have been made Programme Controller. Of course I wanted the job, but life was not as simple as that for me at this time. I was in love and I was teetering on the edge of marriage.

A wonderful girl from Bordeaux, Anna Charron was 21 and fifteen years younger than me. She was a dazzling French Catholic girl, so what was she doing, marrying a nice Jewish boy like me? I decided it was all part of some master plan by that great Programme Controller in the sky!

We didn't marry at that time, but I accepted the job and convinced Anna that she would love Newcastle-upon-Tyne. We moved into a swish modern flat in Gosforth Park overlooking a huge moorland area. It was strange coming back to City Road and walking into the studios as the boss, but some of my pals were still there and I thought that nothing had changed. I'd imagined that somehow it would still be a tight family, but my mentor Bill Lyon Shaw, the previous controller, had left television to run a string of hotels in Devon and although 'Mr George' and 'Mr Alfred' were still directors of the company, they were now greatly removed from the day-to-day running of programmes.

The years had passed by and Tyne Tees had grown up from a small family company to become a major regional television station with networking responsibilities and no more *One O'clock Show*. They had not been making many local entertainment programmes at all and I realised why Tony Jelly had thought of me for the job. I was to revive the 'jolly stuff' as a mixture with all the hard and sometimes grey current affairs programmes that had filled the company's schedules.

Anna and I got married in London on 10 April 1969, and in spite of what Brian Tesler thought, she was not pregnant! We did it the posh way, just because we wanted to.

The wedding day was a bit like my Barmitzvah, only this time I had to make a speech in English and French, because although Anna was fluent in English, her family were not. I remember writing it out in phonetic French and recording it onto tape and then playing it over and over again while we drove down from Newcastle. Jim Nurse, in charge of selling advertising at Tyne Tees and my pal, was my best man and we had some very tricky arrangements to make because there were going to be three totally different types of people at the evening party, which was going to be held in the elegant Italian Room beneath the White House at the end of Great Portland Street.

First there would be my Jewish family and then there were all my pals from the industry, Marty Feldman, Des O'Connor, David Jacobs, Brian and Audrey Tesler, Paul's brother Mike McCartney and his group 'The Scaffold', and the record producer Mel Collins and his wife Jill, who had introduced Anna to me almost a year earlier. Finally, of course, there would be Anna's family from Bordeaux.

All these people were used to entirely different lifestyles and we wanted to make sure that everyone would have a good time. First we had the Malcolm Mitchell Trio to play 'middle of the road' stuff for the first two hours and then 'The Scaffold' with three 100 watt speakers took over. We also had three different menus: the sitdown traditional fare for the families, a stand-up cosmopolitan boozy buffet for the showbiz folk and a disco hamburger bar for those youngsters who wanted to dance.

I remember clearly one particular incident from my wedding concerning the comedian Marty Feldman. As the evening progressed and much drink flowed, Marty hid away in a corner with a few friends and had his drinks and wedding cake.

He was deep into telling a story when one of my cheeky cousins interrupted him in full flow by demanding an autograph. Marty asked him to hang on a minute while he finished his story. I heard the crash as one of my larger drunk uncles tipped over Marty's table, picked him up by the neck and was very busy shaking him like a rag doll. This distant relative was apparently incensed by having his little darling kept waiting for a few moments and it took two other cousins and an aunt to pull him off a very bewildered Marty who by that time was getting very short of air.

He told me as he made his hasty departure that he didn't realise that wedding parties could be so dangerous.

My father was bemused and intrigued by it all and my mother was always just a fraction away from hysterics, so much so that I remember suggesting that she should go out and see a good film at the nearest cinema! It had to be love I thought, because nobody would do this just for fun!

Fun was my business, however, and back in Newcastle I settled into the job. My main problem was that Anna hated the North-East and vowed that she would go out only when we left for London. She hated the food and the weather, she didn't have any good friends and she was not at all interested in television. By 1970, however, we had a beautiful little girl called Manuela Isabelle. That's what happens when you don't watch television.

Perhaps I really was growing up at last, but I was still obsessed with television programmes. I threw myself completely into the job and was very lucky that Chris Palmer, whom I knew very well from my earlier time with the company, agreed to be my second-in-command and take charge of all production. Chris had been a senior cameraman and then a director; he knew his job and together we went on to develop a lot of new projects.

First we launched two new children's series, then a new nightclub series with Norman Vaughan, following that with a new song and dance series starring Cliff Richard. A brilliant Tyne Tees director, Bob Tyrell, made a documentary based on ship building that won an Emmy in New York and then made another award-winning documentary on the life and work of the painter L. S. Lowry. We also made a 'walk about' series with a character called Monty Modlyn who had worked only in radio and was very different and funny in his approach to the Geordie Life. I suppose we were almost overworking the system but the programmes were pouring out and into our schedules. Our local audience ratings were starting to show our own studio-made programmes in the top ten charts, while the atmosphere in the studio was buoyant with the new found confidence in our programmes.

On one occasion a features producer, Frank Entwhistle, came into my office and said that he thought he could get Prince Philip to appear on our *Face the Press* programme. I knew that whenever producers promise to deliver people like Prince Philip, you usually sniff for any alcohol and then tell them to come back with any further information as soon as possible, after which you rarely hear from them again.

A few weeks later a slightly flushed but sober Frank came back to me and said that Prince Philip had agreed to appear.

This was a great scoop, but the visit of Prince Philip to the Tyne Tees studios gave me a personal problem because I, as controller of programmes, had to be his host. I had my large office converted into a private reception room for the Prince. Various drinks were laid on as well as a full make-up table with lights and a special make-up chair.

The Prince put his head back on the chair rest and looked into the make-up girl's eyes and I saw that her hands were shaking. She said, 'This will not take long, sir,' and shakily started.

The Prince, with a great smile, said, 'That's all right, but just don't make me up to look like a middle-aged poof!'

He was ready for the programme in no time but there was a studio delay and we were alone. I had been told by the prince's equerry that the visit was informal, but how informal should you be with Prince Philip? I had done my homework and was determined not to look like a dummy, so I turned to him and said, 'We have something in common, Sir.' It is fair to say that he was puzzled and waited without saying anything, so I ploughed on, sorry I had ever started.

I cleared my throat. 'Yes sir, we both have Russian grandmothers!'

I omitted to say that his was the Czarina and mine was not quite in that category. Happily I was quickly rescued as the studio director arrived to say that the studio was ready.

It was Prince Philip's first live television appearance and he was superb. The programme was part of a networked series presented by Ludovic Kennedy called *Face the Press*, and it made the national newspapers. We were getting Tyne Tees, or 'Tiny Tees' as the Americans called us with affection, well noticed!

It was after that that I took Anna on an extended holiday to France for nearly a month. Although I had been in regular telephone contact with Chris Palmer, who was holding the fort in my absence, I was not prepared for his gloom and depression when I arrived back. Apparently as soon as I had gone he was called over to the managing director's office and hauled over the coals for all the programmes we were making. I was amazed since I had daily meetings with the MD and there was no hint of a disagreement with our output, so what had brought all this on? It was then I realised that Tony Jelly did not share my love for the programming side of the business. His was the world of the boardroom and the politics of the industry, and he had a new dream that Tyne Tees would merge with our neighbour and major station, Yorkshire Television. In theory there was nothing wrong with that except for the fact that our holding company would have to control the finances of both Tyne Tees and Yorkshire and a joint income meant that the two companies would have to schedule their programmes on a compatible basis. It also meant that we should make the minimum of programmes ourselves, relying instead more on the network, with Yorkshire in particular in mind. That was why Tony Jelly suddenly found that he didn't want us to make any more light entertainment programmes. He quickly cut all the programme budgets and we were back to square one.

His move put me on course for a head-on collision with Yorkshire's MD, Ward Thomas, and their controller of programmes, Donald Baverstock.

The crunch came when Ward Thomas called me to a joint scheduling meeting at his office at the Yorkshire Television studios in Leeds. I telephoned him to say that I did not work for Yorkshire Television and had absolutely no intention of being at any meeting at Leeds. I also pointed out that Tyne Tees did not have a management office in Leeds and I did not foresee any plans to visit there in the future. Although I still had three more years to run on my contract I decided that both I and certainly Anna would be better off back in London. I had spoken to Brian Tesler and he suggested that I do the best financial deal possible, finish off my contract and look around for something new in the south.

The problem was that I was a controller of programmes and there were only so many jobs in that category in commercial television; in fact there were only two in London. One was held by Cyril Bennett as controller for London Weekend Television and the other by Brian for Thames Television, who told me straightaway that I certainly wasn't getting his job!

Cyril Bennett was a very good controller at London Weekend and we knew each other well. He called me down and asked whether I would like to be his deputy. It was very tempting as LWT was a very good and happy company and I went back to discuss the offer with Anna. Yet I was also drawn to the idea of going back to producing and directing. It wasn't Godlike but it certainly was a lot more fun.

This point was driven home when Cyril Bennett tragically committed suicide. The whole industry was shocked by his death as he had been well respected and liked. I remember that during my last meeting with Cyril, he had said that I was taking everything much too seriously. 'After all,' he said, 'it's only television.'

Brian Tesler made my mind up for me with a wonderful offer of a job at Thames Television. At Thames, all my old friends were in charge. Philip Jones was Controller of Light Entertainment, Brian Tesler was the Director of Programmes and Howard Thomas was the Managing Director.

All that would have been tempting enough, but the deciding

factor was that Brian wanted me to produce *This Is Your Life*, which was going to be presented once again by Eamonn Andrews.

That was an offer I couldn't refuse.

I did my deal with Tony Jelly and Tyne Tees and left in a sad and strange way. Because of the tricky deal that was just going through with Yorkshire Television, Tony did not want to draw the attention of the Broadcasting Authority to the fact that just as the merger was going ahead, the Controller of Programmes was leaving! It would look as though Yorkshire Television was taking over, and it was important that it did not look that way. So instead of saying goodbye to all my old friends, part of the deal was that I take an extended holiday and after a month, after the financial holding company was established, the announcement about me would be made.

It was all a bit sad for me and for Tyne Tees, because it was one of the best television companies I have ever worked for. There are many 'ifs' to be considered: if George and Alfred had not withdrawn from overseeing the programmes, if Tony Jelly had been more interested in the actual television side of the business, if Anna had been happy in Newcastle, perhaps I would have fought a little harder with Tony Jelly and Ward Thomas. But if all the 'ifs' had happened, then Anna, Manuela and I wouldn't have found such a lovely home in Claygate and our son Gregory wouldn't have been born in St Teresa's Maternity Hospital in Wimbledon in 1972.

13 104 Lives

Apart from the sadness of not saying goodbye to all my friends at Tyne Tees, I felt a wonderful feeling of relief as Anna, eight-month-old Manuela and I drove south. It had been a wonderful three years for me in Newcastle and I had had useful experience in running a large television company. I had also spent a lot of time in London, buying programmes from people such as Lew Grade and was also a member of the television committee that had all regional programme controllers meeting monthly to liaise about their schedules. I would also represent Tony Jelly at the industry's meeting of all the managing directors. Just to be sitting at the same table with the most senior men from Granada, London Weekend, Central, Thames and Yorkshire Television was a fantastic experience for someone who in reality was still a junior participant.

The first thing I did on coming to the south was to buy a house in Claygate. It was a perfect place to bring up an eight-month-old daughter and a new baby which wasn't due to arrive until the following year. And then there was a wonderful reunion with Eamonn Andrews on *This Is Your Life*. It was hard to believe that the programme I had photographed back at the BBC in 1956 was now my responsibility. I knew most of the team, which was headed by Tom Brennand and Roy Bottomley, the writers and programme consultants, and we had worked together with Eamonn Andrews before so it was a pleasure to see them again.

The week before we were due to sit down to discuss the new series, Bob Tyrell from Tyne Tees telephoned me and asked for an urgent meeting. We met in a pub just off the Euston Road. I spotted him at the end of the bar, but he looked ill and haggard. Here was a young man I had known two years earlier as a confident award-winning producer and director.

'What on earth has happened?' I asked him.

'*This Is Your Life* will kill you,' he replied and went on, 'The programme is a nightmare, it's impossible and so is Eamonn!'

It seemed that Eamonn and Bob did not hit it off and he went on.

'Tom and Roy are also impossible,' he warned me, and told me to stay away from the programme. Bob had been working on the first 26 programmes and it had been a terrible experience for him. He told me that he had been driven to a near-nervous breakdown and it had affected his health and his marriage.

I knew Eamonn was my friend but I also knew what he was like when I wanted him to do something that he did not agree with. I usually won by either bluff, guile, threats or pleading, but the key to getting Eamonn's cooperation was to convince him that I was right. It was the same with Tom and Roy so I thanked Bob Tyrell for his genuine concern, I wished him well for a healthy recovery and reassured him that everything would be all right.

It was more than all right, it was great. I had a formidable team of six researchers, two directors, two production assistants, a programme organiser, a programme secretary and Jack Crawshaw, who researched and wrote his own stories. Jack quickly became invaluable and worked for a while as my associate producer before later taking over as producer on the show himself.

The year was now 1971 and I had 26 programmes to make in my first year. *This Is Your Life* is a very powerful

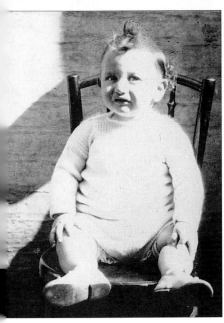

Above An early study taken by my Aunt Rose

Right With my mother, Jessie Morris, 1962

Above Lewis Morris – my father

Right Again, with my mother

Above On honeymoon with Anna in the Bahamas, 1969
Below In New York with Eamonn and his wife, Grainne, 1975

ight My daughter,
anuela, 1992

Below On holiday in
pain with my son,
regory, 1995

Above Filming at Tyne Tees TV with Des O'Connor, 1959

Top right Muhammad Ali, me, Lucille Ball, Eamonn Andrews and Noel Coward, 1965
Bottom right With The Duke of Edinburgh after his first live TV appearance, 1968

Above With Zsa Zsa Gabor, 1964 . . .

Left . . . and again in 1992

Top right With Liz Dawn, *Coronation Street*'s Vera Duckworth, 1995

Bottom right With Pierce Brosnan and Michael Aspel in 1995, plotting a 'hit' on Desmond Llewellyn – 'Q' in the James Bond movies

Left With Ursula
Andress, 1993

Right Bob and Delores
Hope, 1995

Below left Buzz Aldrin,
1994

Below right Jane
Russell, 1995

Left With Michael and the famous Big Red Book, 1988

Right In Hollywood with King Kong, 1989

Below Rehearsing with my son, Gregory, who's standing in for our next subject, William Shatner, in 1989

Left With Margaret Thatcher, recording a message for Jimmy Young, 1985 ...

Below ... and with her *Spitting Image* clone in Montreux, 1989

With John Major, recording a message for cricket umpire Dickie Bird, 1992

With Chaim Herzog, President of Israel, 1985

With Shimon Peres, Prime Minister of Israel, 1985

Left Eamonn clutching a red accounts book ready to pounce on Bill Roache, *Coronation Street*'s Ken Barlow, 198[

Right Achieving a childhood ambition – sitting in a Spitfire, 1993

Bottom left Scheduling the running order for the 1994/95 series – all in code to ensure secrecy

Bottom right Stalking David Hasselhoff on the set of *Baywatch*, 1993

Revisiting old haunts, 1995

and emotional experience for any family to go through. Parents, children, other relatives and friends have been known to come together afterwards in a way that had not existed before the show. Such power however can also work in reverse and one such story was of a man who was a hero both to his family and the village in which they lived.

It is always great to find an unknown person and for very good reasons feature them and pay them the tribute that they deserve on the programme.

No better story existed than the one we were pursuing on my first series in 1971. He was a true hero. He was one of a pair of twins who were both merchant seamen in the war. One died just after the war and one went on to tell his story for the years that followed.

He had been torpedoed in the North Sea around March 1942 and, thrown into the icy water, was unlikely to last for more than a few minutes. He was lucky, however, because among their escort ships was an American corvette that was first on the scene. A boat was lowered and our friend was plucked out of the water at the very last minute by, as he remembered, a 'red headed sailor' who turned out to be the ship's doctor. He was saved.

We decided to go ahead with the story and made our usual arrangements with all his family and closest friends who were told to keep our plans a secret from him. If he found out we would, as always, have to cancel the programme. A researcher was told that we must, just must find that anonymous American doctor. We were talking about 29 years ago and we didn't know the name of the American ship or the exact date – and we couldn't ask the best person who had this information!

Department of War archives can be helpful if you have some information to give them, but no records were kept in the English archives of American ships in the war. The search and the weeks went on, the American war archivists were interviewed and eventually the American ship's name was discovered. The crew's names and jobs were examined and, yes, they had the name of the ship's doctor. They couldn't tell us the colour of his hair but they knew that he lived in Chicago during 1950.

Our researcher went over to America and examined the medical lists of doctors who had been in the navy at that time; it took a month and only a week before the programme did we come across his new address in Pennsylvania! A phone number was found and I telephoned it to be told that he had just moved, but they had a forwarding address in Philadelphia!

It was two days before the programme when I got him on the telephone. The whole team gathered around as I asked him whether he remembered the event. The suspense was tremendous as he said to me, 'Of course I remember! It's not every day that you pull someone out of the sea, seconds before they are about to die!'

He was curious as to how we found him and I asked him about his red hair; he said that he had lost most of it. I told him about our programme and then said, 'So, Doctor, will you come over to appear on Paul's life?' He was delighted and said, 'I'd be honoured to be part of Pat's programme.'

'That's great,' I said giving the thumbs up to the team who all applauded.

'But,' I continued, 'it's not Pat, it's Paul.'

'No it isn't,' he said. 'It's not a name I will ever forget.'

Then I realised that it was Pat and not Paul who had been torpedoed. Paul had taken the story as his own – a good tale to tell after his brother's death. No real harm in that, he must have thought, when he told the story to the girl he was eventually to marry. But as the years matured, so did the story until it became the focal point of his family. He was a hero to them and to the small village that they lived in.

By doing his life we would be unable to stop the truth coming out to the whole village and our audience of many millions. Paul's myth would be destroyed and so would he, when everyone knew the truth. We didn't of course tell the family why, but we cancelled the programme at the last minute. The American doctor was told that we were cancelling for family reasons. I don't know whether he ever guessed the truth. Nearly six months' work was thrown away on the programme, but that was better than ruining someone's life!

Another disaster was narrowly avoided when the family of a famous personality was being entertained in a suite at a secret hotel in London on the night before the programme. I was late for the get-together and was in the hotel lobby, asking for the number of the room that we had booked for the family. I was given the number of the room and as I turned, there in front of me stood the subject himself.

He had just arrived in that very hotel to wine and dine with an attractive lady that I knew was not his wife because I had her and all their relatives a few feet above his head! He and the lady went over to a dark corner of the bar to continue their intimate conversation and I recovered from being a marble statue and rushed upstairs to the suite where I told everyone that there was a press party downstairs and they would certainly guess what was up. The family was spirited away down the back stairs to another hotel and we made the programme the following evening.

Some years later I told the story to the personality concerned and he blushed then assured me that the meeting was the last before he went back to the bosom of his family.

I believed him . . . wouldn't you?

We also lost programmes because the subjects occasionally guessed what was up.

Ronnie Barker was worried as for over three weeks his wife had been putting the telephone down whenever he walked into the room. When Ronnie asked who it was, he was always greeted by a pause before some implausible answer. Was his wife having an affair? He couldn't believe it until he was outside their bedroom and she was on the telephone again. He approached the open door as quickly as he could but she heard him and put the telephone down, hiding a small card in her dressing table drawer.

Ronnie waited until she had left the room, then, feeling very guilty, he opened the drawer, went through her underwear and found the card. It was a plain white card with just the name 'Brian' and a telephone number. Ronnie took a deep breath and rang the number.

'Hello, *This Is Your Life*, can I help you,' said Brian our researcher working on Ronnie's programme.

The programme was dead from that moment on and we have never done Ronnie Barker's life, but we have changed our telephone policy.

From then on the very first thing a researcher is told on joining the programme is that we never, NEVER, answer the telephone by giving the name of the programme. It's much quicker to cancel the programme by telling the subject directly, which is what our researcher Tom Wettengel did when he rang the actress Elaine Stritch. He was ringing her husband to get his permission to do the programme, when the deep male voice answered the phone. Tom introduced himself and went on to describe what we had in mind.

'Well, that's swell honey, go ahead, but this is Elaine Stritch talking. Don't you usually keep it a secret?'

Tom was stopped dead and so were we!

There is no doubt in my mind as to who the luckiest researcher on the programme was. Maurice Leonard, now a producer, was then a humble researcher who was sent out to London Airport to meet the beautiful actress Ursula Andress, who was appearing as a guest on Charles Aznavour's *Life*. So keen was he to help her that, waving away the porters, he alone lifted her luggage into the car boot, only to feel his back go!

Ms Andress is a handy lady and when they arrived at the studios I found Maurice without his shirt, face-down on Ursula's lap having his back massaged. I don't know if the massage helped his back but he has lived off the story ever since!

The very tightest of secrets can sometimes get out in the strangest way. The first transmission of *This Is Your Life* by Thames was from the London Palladium. The date was 1969 and it was also the first night of Des O'Connor's stage show. Before the curtain was due to go up, Des got very nervous and decided to go outside to get some air. He stood at the back of the theatre and just stared at the traffic. Then he saw a large coach slowly driving past. Although the coach was only dimly lit, he was sure that he saw his entire family passing before his eyes: uncles, aunts and some relatives he had not seen in years. He said later the experience was like the one you have when you're drowning and your life flashes before you. He vowed at the time never to have a drink before a performance again and shrugged it off.

That was until he saw Eamonn step on to the stage from behind the scenery and say: 'Des O'Connor, This Is Your Life.'

The programme can be a terrible strain on those who have to keep the secret from their partner, because sometimes they are just not used to telling lies. In 1973 we planned to feature Douglas Fairbanks Junior, so we contacted his sweet wife. She gave us her blessing to go ahead and we sent a researcher to Hollywood to work on the story. Then a doctor rang me in my office. He told me that he was Mrs Fairbanks' doctor and that she was ill through the strain of keeping this secret from her husband. He gave me an ultimatum; either we told Douglas Fairbanks of our plans and did the programme, or we cancelled. He would not be responsible if Mrs Fairbanks had a breakdown because of me.

We cancelled immediately and it took another sixteen years before we succeeded in doing Douglas Fairbanks' *Life*.

* * *

It occasionally happens that the subject experiences cold feet on appearing on a programme devoted to them. Danny Blanchflower achieved immortality the evening he left Eamonn Andrews holding on to his coat as he slipped out, said 'No' and made a successful getaway, running off along a street. That was back in 1956. Eighteen years later, at the beginning of a live programme that I was directing, Richard Gordon, of the 'Doctor' books and films fame, came into Thames Television reception in London. Suddenly Eamonn Andrews appeared behind him.

As he saw Eamonn, Richard also spotted two cameras in the corridor.

'Hello,' said Eamonn. 'Tonight, Richard Gordon, this is your life.'

Richard looked at Eamonn. 'Are we on now?' he asked.

'Yes,' said Eamonn, 'this is live.'

'Balls,' said Richard. He then turned to dash out of the building.

'We've got a lot of guests waiting to see you,' said Eamonn rather anxiously.

'I didn't invite them,' replied Richard.

By this time I had faded the picture out and started a stand-by programme on actor Sam Kydd, due to have gone out the following week.

Richard Gordon was now halfway out of the studio door.

'Oh, come on,' said Eamonn.

Richard paused. 'Oh, all right,' he said.

He went back into the studio with Eamonn and we recorded the programme for the following week.

I don't know why Richard Gordon said no in the first place, but what I do know is that he made the front page of nearly every newspaper in the country on the following day.

We occasionally made a programme outside the studios, if the situation demanded it. Michael Wood worked with the flying doctor service in East Africa. He did such a good job that he became very much a local legend so we decided to devote a programme to his life.

In 1972 my team flew to Nairobi and then travelled for many miles by truck to a Masai village where the doctor was due to land his small plane and hold one of his regular clinics for the villagers. We had arranged for one of his partners to take over the clinic after we threw our surprise. All went well and Eamonn came out from behind some bushes and presented the Red Book to the rather bemused doctor who just stared at Eamonn when he said: 'Michael Wood, this is your life.'

He proved to be a good sport and came back with us to Nairobi Airport in order to fly back with us to do the programme back in London. Everything had been arranged, and Eamonn and Michael boarded the plane followed by the crew and finally myself, only I was stopped by the guard who insisted that the plane was now full. Showing him my reserved ticket made no impression because the guard insisted that Mr Morris was already on the plane. As he was carrying a rather large gun and I was getting nowhere, I told the others to go ahead and the plane took off. I then asked if there were any other planes in the airport and they pointed to one on the runway.

'I'll take that one,' I shouted, and ran to the plane, waving my ticket in the air. I got on and the 747 took off. I made my way to an empty seat, waited until we were airborne and called the hostess over.

'Where does this plane go to?' I asked her. Other passengers looked at me strangely.

'Entebbe,' she said.

'And after that?'

'Libya.'

'And after that?'

'Rome.'

That was close enough for me. I changed at Rome and much to the surprise of Eamonn and the team, who didn't expect to see me again, I arrived at the studio only six hours late, just in time to make the London end of the programme.

Producing the *This Is Your Life* on cricketer Ray Illingworth, I agreed with my researcher that I would film a special message from the writer J. B. Priestley. I was going to direct this piece because I had heard that 'J.B.' could be difficult if he chose, but on the day he was fine and graciously offered me a glass of sherry while the crew fixed up the lights and their cameras. Suddenly he leaned forward and said that he wanted to ask me something.

Overawed by the great man I sat and nodded with apprehension. 'Of course,' I said.

'I hate filming you know. I like Ray, he's a great man, but I hate filming. Tell me,' he said, moving even closer, 'what's the name of the programme this is for?' I was about to tell him when he went on, 'I hate that programme – what's it called?'

I waited, knowing what was to come.

'You know, *This Is Your Life*. Now I would never film for that.'

'Right,' I said, nodding my head and smiling with understanding.

'Tell me,' he went on, 'I didn't catch the name of the programme this is for.'

I swallowed my sherry. 'It's a tribute, a special tribute to Ray Illingworth.'

'Yes, but what do I look for in the *Radio Times*?'

The lights and camera were ready, saving me from more ridiculous avoidance.

We finished filming and J.B. was very good but still puzzled. 'What do I look out for?' he asked as we stood at his door.

'Oh, we can do better than that,' I said generously. 'I will send you your own copy of the programme on tape.' I shook his hand as he prepared his next obvious and repetitive question. 'And,' I said, 'I want to thank you personally and say what a pleasure it has been to meet you.' With that I was off.

Some years ago we did a *Life* on an air sea rescue man. The programme was recorded as it was to be shown on television six weeks later, yet within a few days I was phoned by the subject to tell me that his mother, who had appeared on the programme, was in fact very ill and was not expected to survive for more than a few days. He went on to explain that it was her dearest wish to see her son's programme.

I was moved by this and offered to arrange for a special recording of the programme to be taken to the hospital for her bedside viewing, but I was told that this was no good because she wanted to see it go out in the normal way, so all her friends could see it at the same time. I realised that this was no ego trip but a very proud mother who wanted all her friends and relations to see her son receive his honour, but explained to the son that the scheduling of that programme was outside my control, but I could manage to move the schedule forward by three weeks.

He was grateful but explained that she had only days to go.

Sadly there was nothing else I could do, yet his mother held on for the three weeks against all the doctors' forecasts and refused to die until the day after the transmission was broadcast.

Mothers are very important to *This Is Your Life*. When the Red Book was shown to Warren Mitchell, Warren, who is not shy, said in character, 'Bloody hell, I would tell you to sod off but I know my mother will love it.'

That wasn't the only problem with Warren's programme. As luck would have it, we had a major technical breakdown which delayed the recording of the programme by an hour and a half. Booked live onto a special line from Munich was Richard Burton, a great pal of Warren's. When the time arrived, we went over to Munich and the waiting Richard Burton.

Warren was surprised and then looked more closely at the incoming television feed. 'You're pissed,' he said to Richard.

'So would you be, you old fart, if you had been stuck for an hour and a half waiting for this damned show.'

So much for the dialogue of the luvvies.

In December 1972, Anna went into hospital to have Gregory and I was determined to be present at the birth. During the delivery the obstetrician, perhaps in order to relax me, decided to engage in conversation. He told me that he realised that I produced *This Is Your Life* and would I mind if he asked me a question? He was right in the middle of the delivery at the time and I was in no position to deny him anything.

'When are you going to run out of people?' he said.

I stared at Gregory's head that was just emerging and told him the truth.

'As long as you keep delivering them, we'll keep telling their stories!'

It took four series, that's 104 programmes, before I decided to say goodbye to Eamonn and the team. I felt it was time for another change. I was determined to go out with a bang this time and decided that we should reverse the programme and do a *Life* on Eamonn himself. It took a lot of persuading because the team did not think that we would succeed in keeping it a secret from the man himself, but I promised them that I would come up with something that would fool even Eamonn.

David Nixon, the TV magician, was a very good friend of Eamonn's and was delighted to be the presenter. He also agreed to invite Eamonn onto a 'dummy' *David Nixon Show* on the pretext of getting Eamonn to do a guest spot and be sawn in half.

Meanwhile Jack Crawshaw and I went to Ireland and secretly met Eamonn's wife Grainne in a Dublin hotel. As luck would have it, a friend saw me with Grainne and started the rumour that Grainne and I were having an affair. This was then confirmed by Grainne's and Eamonn's children, Emma and Naimh, who later said on a BBC interview, 'Oh yes, we heard that Malcolm was having an affair with Mummy.'

What I was doing was setting up the most fantastic bluff that the *Life* team had ever done. First we invented a mythical Indian doctor who was so saintly that he made Mother Teresa seem quite sinful in comparison. The problem was that a dummy script had to be written to convince Eamonn that we were going to do the programme on the Wednesday when in fact we were planning the 'real' show for the night before, when Eamonn was to guest on the *David Nixon Show*.

That began to become problematic as we got nearer to the programme. Eamonn was insisting on seeing the research for the programme – which of course did not exist. On Tuesday, the actual day of Eamonn's *Life*, he telephoned me to give me a terrible rollicking because the script had still not turned up, although I had promised he would have it the night before. He demanded to speak to Jack Crawshaw or anyone in the office who could give him some more information. In fact the office was totally empty because the team was in the studio, setting up the programme.

I remember looking around at the empty desks and saying, 'My God, it's chaos here! I can't get anyone right now, we are in the middle of a terrible rush and are due to have a programme meeting right now. I must go. Goodbye!'

My master stroke was still to come. I was sure that if any suspicions were lurking in Eamonn's mind they would be settled if he knew that Grainne was in Dublin just before he set out for the *David Nixon Show*. He knew we would never do the programme without his wife being there, so I came to an arrangement with a telephone operator who 'fixed' Eamonn's telephone at 6.30 p.m. for ten minutes. Any number dialled on his telephone during that time would go through to a special telephone at our Teddington studios.

As we set out for David's show I told Eamonn that there had been a message for him to ring Grainne in Dublin that evening. He told me he would do it later but I nagged until he agreed. He dialled his Dublin number and spoke to Grainne in Teddington, who gave him the day's news and told him that they had been invited to a party on the Saturday night and should she accept?

Once that domestic exchange had taken place he relaxed; he just positively knew that it was not going to be his life.

Once David had shown Eamonn the book and Grainne had walked out to greet him, Eamonn spotted me standing at the back of the cameras. I gave him a wink and a shrug. It was my way of saying goodbye.

14 Opportunity Knocks

During my last year on *This Is Your Life* it became very obvious that Jack Crawshaw was ready for more responsibility and I thought it a good idea if he produced the series, with me as the executive producer to oversee the handover. It worked well. Jack did a superb job, leaving me free to assist Philip Jones in running what had become the most successful light entertainment department in the country.

The year was 1974 and Thames Television's light entertainment programmes were all in the top ten national ratings. *This Is Your Life* was usually number one, with *Man About the House*, *George and Mildred*, *And Father Makes Three*, *Bless This House*, *Robin's Nest*, *Nearest and Dearest*, *The Benny Hill Show*, *Whodunnit?* and Hughie Green's *Opportunity Knocks* all watched by millions of people throughout the country.

Philip, who was running the department singlehandedly, did not have a smooth relationship with Hughie Green, who could be difficult to handle at times. He suggested that I become the executive producer on *Opportunity Knocks* together with *This Is Your Life* and also produce and direct the annual *TV Times Awards*.

I was sliding into the management side of the business again, but I agreed. Back in 1955 I had photographed an early quiz series called *Double Your Money* that Hughie Green presented; I liked him then and got on with him very well. I also enjoyed *Opportunity Knocks*, but knew there was always a battle between Hughie and the company because he was always pushing the system to do programmes in his way and this did not always fit in with Philip's ideas.

I would pour oil on the production waters and we just about got through it. Philip Jones was not a confrontational sort of person and would get very upset indeed after a battle with Hughie. After a while things got so bad that Hughie threatened to sue Thames. I suggested to Philip that we should part company with Hughie unless he got another person to present the programme and withdrew from his weekly participation. All of that was highly unlikely; the pity of it all was that Hughie was right in principle most of the time. Hughie would just not calm down and it became inevitable that he would eventually leave. I was sad to see him go. I enjoyed his company and I learnt a lot from him.

About this time I met up with Lance Percival and Jeremy Lloyd, who had an idea for a crime quiz. They asked for my help and together we developed a new programme called *Whodunnit?* The programme began with a crime, and then all the participants came on to the game part of the show and were quizzed by a celebrity panel who had to find out 'whodunnit'. The crime stories would usually take about twenty minutes and I had a chance to write some of them.

Luckily for us the programme did well, with Edward Woodward as the host who eventually handed over to my old pal from the *Can Do* days way back in 1957, Jon Pertwee, who really made the programme his own. It was never out of the top ten ratings in its six-year run.

A few weeks after *Whodunnit?* hit the TV screens Gregory decided to have the mumps. All the family were immune for various reasons except me, because as a child I had contracted absolutely nothing. I had never been ill or spent any time in any hospital, so I caught a very mild form of mumps from dear Greg. Nothing swelled up but I had a sore throat, which meant I couldn't go to work and spent two weeks in bed at

home for the first time in my life. For some reason, probably
boredom, I decided to watch the Thames output during the
day for the first time. I saw it from a new viewpoint and
wrote a letter expressing my feelings to Jeremy Isaacs, who
was the new controller of programmes for Thames, Brian
Tesler having moved on to become the managing director of
London Weekend Television.

I thought no more about the letter and after all the tablets
and TLC from Anna I eventually returned to my production
office at Teddington with no further ill effects. On my arrival
I found a memo from Jeremy Isaacs on my desk, thanking
me for my letter and asking me to a lunch meeting to discuss
my points in a little more detail. Frankly I did not have any
more detail; it was a note written as a basic reaction to our
daytime programmes. My simplistic thoughts, however, did
not put Jeremy off, for he wanted me to join him as the
administrative controller of the programme department.
Over lunch he told me that Jack Andrews, the present controller, was thinking of moving on to production. Therefore
it made sense that someone with my experience should take
his place; in fact I would be swapping jobs with him.

I wasn't at all sure that I was getting the better part of this
'swap', but Jeremy was very persuasive and wooed me with
more money and a company car. I told him that I knew
nothing about administration and confessed my secret: I was
really only a programme 'hack', good at making a certain
type of programme and nothing else. He was not to be put
off, so in 1975 I became the controller of administration for
the programme department for Thames Television, one of
the largest commercial television companies.

My responsibilities covered a budget output that
amounted to 30 million pounds! I became involved with
every programme department, every programme union dis-
pute, personnel problems, programme contracts, staff
contracts and began to be involved with the problems of
some of the two thousand people who worked for the

company . . . how did I get into this terrible job? It was new and demanding, and I found myself working long hours.

My new office was in the Euston Road while with my family I had moved out to Godalming where Anna had found a fantastic seventeenth-century coach house, complete with full length thick oak beams and twenty inch thick stone walls surrounded by two acres of ground going down to the River Wey, a conservatory, a boat house, a well, a small natural pond and a summer house. The house had 23 rooms, including a lift and galleried hall.

What was an ex-hairdresser from the Caledonian Road doing with all this?

Everything has its drawbacks though. It took me an hour and a half to drive into town and an hour and a half to get back again! I spent the next few years just travelling three hours a day before doing any work at all. By the time I got home at night I was in no condition to live a civilised life, let alone stay awake!

It was at about this time that Thames decided on a rather audacious plan to sell its programmes and formats to America. The plan was to take over a whole New York television station for two weeks and put on all Thames programmes, from six o'clock in the evening right through until three o'clock the next morning. Channel Nine, WOR, was chosen, and I was asked to go over and oversee the plan. It was also decided that while I was there, I would produce a nightly live talk show between New York and London. Eamonn was to go on in New York and I chose Dick Cavett to go to London.

Channel Nine, WORTV, like a lot of non-network television stations in New York, was an efficient but small operation. It was situated on Times Square, above a soft porn cinema. The evening show with Eamonn and Dick Cavett was launched and got off to a tremendous start by having a live three-way link-up between Debbie Reynolds in New York, Carrol O'Connor in Los Angeles and Warren

Mitchell in London. The topic was Johnny Speight's BBC series that Warren Mitchell starred in, called *Till Death Us Do Part*, and its American copy, *Archie Bunker's*. Warren Mitchell's Alf Garnett role was played in the US by Carrol O'Connor.

Carrol O'Connor is a distinguished American actor and he did not take kindly to Warren sliding into his Alf Garnett persona and calling the American version 'a lot of old bloody rubbish'. Debbie Reynolds was incensed by Warren's language and threatened to walk off the programme, while Carrol pretended his 'earpiece' had failed and he couldn't hear anything. Eamonn in New York and Dick in London were having great difficulty in controlling things and the effect was exciting but chaotic. The British press, who had spent years knocking the Sunday night *Eamonn Andrews Show*, had a field day by proclaiming: 'Here we go again!'

It settled down but was always dangerous, which is the way Eamonn liked to work. I remained very busy running the station. I took a small apartment on 55th Street because I wanted to actually live in New York as opposed to staying in a hotel. Just the thought that you could ring down to the deli for a salt beef sandwich at three o'clock in the morning made me realise that I was a long way from Godalming, Anna, Manuela, Gregory and the three cats! I didn't realise at the time but prolonged absence was not doing my marriage any good.

On my return to London I was told I was going to be offered the job of deputy controller of programmes for Thames. It was flattering but I was secretly horrified. I had no doubt that I could do it, but by that time we had a new managing director called Bryan Cowgill. Although Bryan loved the business of television, he would not fall in love with Jeremy, and I knew who would end up as piggy in the middle.

Some instinct told me not to take up the offer and I delayed in accepting. It was just as well that I had because within a month, Jeremy did leave and later went on to become the head of a new television service, Channel Four. That left just the Managing Director and me, and Bryan Cowgill was a good television man who loved the business. He was also very good company to share a drink with, but he got bored with the bureaucracy of the job and loved to do some of the interesting things that I was doing, leaving the nasty grey bits for me.

At this time commercial television, as an industry, went through its own sort of menopause. People of my age who had joined at the start of commercial television back in 1956 were all now fast approaching 50. Some had become the heavy drinkers I had met over the years, others had simply stayed in the same job for too long. The divorces, mortgages and redundancies, and perhaps some faded dreams were all taking their toll and it was the same throughout the network. Thames as an example began to have an abnormal series of early deaths and suicides over a period of two years.

One producer hanged himself in a garage, another producer threw himself in front of a train, someone else, who was due to meet me to discuss his financial settlement with the company, just went on up to the top of the building and jumped off. There were several nervous breakdowns, then the controller of the outside broadcast department died, and shortly afterwards his replacement also died and unbelievably his deputy of 34 also died suddenly from complications during an attack of pleurisy.

To complete the picture, my father died, and this marked a turning point in my life. I decided that I should do what I enjoyed doing and that was making programmes. It would also mean that I could work again from Teddington, which was only a 40 minute drive away from my house. It was clear to me that I should start paying a lot more attention to my marriage.

I asked Bryan Cowgill to replace me and in 1979 I returned to being a producer with the light entertainment department. I was pleased to work for Philip Jones once again, although I realised I had not directed a programme for over five years. Could I still do it at 47? I remembered that when we had all joined television in 1956, we said that we would be out at 35 – something about reflexes and nervous tension being a young man's job . . . Was I making the right decision in going back or was this the 'mid life' crisis that people spoke about?

I really didn't know. All I knew was that I was going to have a great time once again. Little did I realise that that was only the half of it.

15 Once More into the Breach, Dear Friends

I t was good to be back at the Teddington studios. I was busy doing a quiz programme with Benny Green and also preparing for another *TV Times Award* programme. The awards were always good fun to do because they were contained in an hour-long show with live music and a few guest spots.

That particular year there was a special award for a new American series called *Buck Rogers in the 21st Century*. The American star, Gil Gerrard, had agreed to come over, which was great, but I knew from my Mayfair cinema days that the original Buck Rogers was played by Buster Crabbe, who had also played Flash Gordon. Doing a bit of my own research I found out that Buster Crabbe was a very fit 80-year-old living in California, so I invited him on the programme to do a double act with Gil. After the programme I spent a wonderful few hours with Buster, reminiscing about the old days. I didn't care that it had cost a small fortune to bring him over and I didn't care that hardly anyone watching the programme would appreciate who he was.

It had taken me 37 years, but I had finally met Flash Gordon in person!

I didn't miss not being part of the management team, except for losing my company car. In compensation I bought a new BMW, which I found to be perfect if a little dull. Maybe I was getting old after all!

With my history of receiving dramatic telephone invitations

I should have known better that sunny afternoon sitting in my Teddington office than to answer my phone, but I did. I was asked to attend a very urgent meeting at the managing director's office that evening. Oh no, not again! I thought. I had been back at Teddington for less than six months, and whatever it was this time, I would say no. Bryan Cowgill had been a programme controller at the BBC, during which time he was mainly responsible for launching the highly successful *Mastermind* series. He had a dream that one day there would be an international version of the programme, and he wanted me to produce and direct it as soon as possible.

It was a marvellous project which had never been done before and it meant a live simultaneous satellite link-up between Britain, Australia and America. The programme would then be transmitted in all three continents. It was to be called *Top of the World* with a potential audience of around 70 million viewers.

I agreed and was delighted to produce this project. Eamonn Andrews was going to present it from London and I had just over seven months to get it ready. I had to hire the technical staff to iron out all the problems, such as delays in sound, and to book four satellites, one over the Indian Ocean, one over the Pacific, the Atlantic and the 'West Star' over America. While all that was going on I had to choose the other studios that would be involved. This meant I had to visit Australia and America as soon as possible.

I spent nearly three weeks in Miami with the public broadcast station PB2. They would handle the contestants their end but I would have to direct their cameras and lighting changes from London. The same situation applied to Australia. The ABC studios in Sydney would be the location for the Australian contestants, with me directing their studios from London. Once the arrangements with the studios were set up, all that remained was getting the right contestants. They all had to be given a common test to enable me to match them up as closely as possible. It was going to be a hard-fought contest and the first prize after the thirteen week run was a specially chosen 1925 vintage Rolls Royce Cabriolet. This prize was valued by Sotheby's at around £35,000; a big enough prize to impress even the Americans.

Once again I was away from Anna and the family. I visited all the large American cities from Miami to Boston, Chicago, New York and Los Angeles, from where I departed for Australia and Sydney, Canberra, Melbourne, Brisbane and Perth. For six weeks I was completely jetlagged. At the end of that stint I did play hookey for a few days by breaking my flight back from Sydney to Los Angeles in Hawaii.

I booked into the Hawaii Hilton, which was situated by a small turquoise cove. Knowing that it was bitterly cold in England I ran down in my trunks to the sandy beach. It was very hot with a cloudless sky overhead and calm warm sea.

I spotted a small raft floating twenty metres into the sea.

The beach was empty as I swam out to the floating raft and sat there with my feet in the water, feeling the sun on my back and thinking that no one in the world knew where I was at that moment.

Just then a Japanese chap swam from out of nowhere and sat on the other end of the raft and asked me a question.

'You're Malcolm Morris, aren't you?'

I looked at him. He was smiling and all I could think was, 'Welcome to the Twilight Zone.' I admitted that I was indeed Malcolm Morris.

'I not forget face,' he said.

'But, but, but ...' I stammered. I was not at my most eloquent.

He put me out of my misery and told me he was with Sony and that he had been part of a party that I had taken around Teddington a few months earlier. How's that for trying to play hookey in the middle of the Pacific!

* * *

The atmosphere was strained when I returned home and when I told Anna that I would be doing the same trip again a few months later, I realised we had reached the point of no return with our marriage. It's amazing how stupid and complacent we can become. I loved Anna very much and she loved me, so what was the problem? The problem was that I was devoting too much time to my work and not enough to my family.

It has been done by others a million times before and since, and we never learn.

Top of the World was not as successful as it should have been. I think it needed a follow-up series to establish it with all the different audiences. Also, Eamonn had insisted on playing the quiz as a game, thus the programme was not as serious as it should have been. Yet directing it for me was one of my most exciting television experiences.

I spent as much time as possible at home after the series was finished and we also took some holidays with the children. We both tried hard to make things work but it was becoming difficult. Anna and I decided that perhaps we were just too far out of town to see friends, have a social life and go out more often, and so we decided to sell the house. We found a very large flat in Roehampton and moved in and then in 1981 bought a villa in Spain.

This Is Your Life continued to remain in the ratings but the programme started to take its toll on Jack Crawshaw who, as the producer, was working too hard. He became ill and then decided that he needed a change and wanted to direct. It was a brave decision as he wanted to leave the programme to be trained as a director. Jack was so highly regarded by the company that he was put on a director's course and taken on by the outside broadcast and sports departments.

I was delighted to be back on the programme again. Eamonn and I had continued to be close friends so it was a very good move for both of us. I knew that making the 26 programmes for that year was going to be tough, but I relished the challenge.

There were three stages involved in a series of *This Is Your Life*. The first part ran from July to September. That's when we looked for and decided who the subjects were going to be for that year. The second part was from October to April when we actually made and transmitted the 26 *Lives*. The third part ran from May to July, when we just tried not to think about the programme or anything at all.

Crazy things continued to happen during the making of the series which do stay in the memory, like the time when we went to Nottingham to surprise the comedian Charlie Williams. Charlie was playing at a large nightclub just outside the city and we arrived at about 11 p.m., just before Charlie was due to finish his act on stage. It was impossible to go inside the club because that would have given the surprise away before we even got anywhere near Charlie, so we hid in a small alleyway around the back of the club. It was dark and cold but we knew we would not have long to wait before the manager, who was in on the secret, would come out the back and take us inside.

As we stood in the darkness we heard someone coming, but it was not the manager. Eamonn quickly hid behind a large rusty sheet of corrugated metal that was held off the ground by two wooden supports. A rather large man lurched around the corner, slightly the worse for a lot of beer, and decided to get rid of some of it against the sheet of metal. He must have drunk a lot of beer because his relief seemed to go on for a very long time, but it was much longer for Eamonn, hiding behind the sheet of metal. His feet, however, were sticking out from the bottom of the corrugated sheet. The great tidal flow went neatly down the corrugations and over Eamonn's feet, filling his shoes and soaking his socks. The man, greatly relieved, returned to the club and didn't hear Eamonn's words which were certainly not suitable for television. I sympathised with Eamonn but the tears coming down my cheeks did not add to my sincerity.

Another time we were hiding in a hotel room in Manchester, waiting to go to the Granada studios to surprise Jack Howarth, who played Albert Tatlock in *Coronation Street*. Our surprise was not due to happen until 10 p.m. because it was too dangerous to go to the studios in case we were spotted, so we waited until most people would have gone home. Since it was a Wednesday and getting near 7 p.m., we decided to watch – what else – a recording of *This Is Your Life*. I ordered two drinks from room service, which arrived just as the programme was starting. It was a Peter Sellers type of waiter who was holding the tray when I opened the door, and of course he would not give it to me but insisted on bringing it in. He leant over to place the tray on the small coffee table when he saw Eamonn sitting there.

He stopped in mid-bend and looked at the television set and then at Eamonn sitting in front of him.

'It's yourself, it is,' he said, as the contents of the tray gently slid into Eamonn's lap.

I think it was the Gaelic that Eamonn used, but I couldn't be sure.

Strangely enough it was some years later when we were back, hiding on the *Coronation Street* set and waiting to spring a surprise on Bill Roache, that one of my greatest fears came true.

We had always joked that one day I would lose the book and earlier I had put it behind the bar of the Rovers Return for safe keeping. I knew that I could reach it very quickly when it was needed.

We got the signal that Bill would be arriving in two minutes for a rehearsal.

I reached behind the bar, but no Red Book came to hand. It had just disappeared from the face of the earth! There was no time to panic or argue with anybody, as Bill was now just over one minute away. Eamonn turned to ask me for the book, but I wasn't there; I was down the corridor and into the accounts office. I saw a red accounts hardback folder and grabbed it, ran back and shoved it into a surprised Eamonn's hands.

'Don't even think about it, just do it!' I bullied.

He did and nobody noticed it wasn't the 'real' Red Book that we used for the surprise. There is usually a short time lapse between the surprise and the body of the actual show, and the book was found before we did the rest.

An enterprising stage manager had put it on another shelf for safety.

This Is Your Life is at its best when doing the life of a non-showbusiness person, and Kitty Wilson was a perfect subject for the programme. Her family had sent us her story and some photographs of her and some of the 50 children she has fostered over the years. Wouldn't it be wonderful if we could find all those children and have a grand reunion after 30 years?

We agreed, and a few weeks later we found ourselves hiding behind some wide posts in Liverpool Street station. Kitty was coming up to town with a friend to do some Christmas shopping and what she wasn't expecting to see was a photograph of her with all her foster children blown up to twenty feet and strung across the platform.

The train pulled in and Eamonn leapt out at Kitty. 'Ah ha!' he said, putting his hand on her shoulder. 'You're not expecting this,' and he brought the book around from behind his back.

The terror on the poor woman's face said it all. Eamonn looked back at me and I shook my head. She did look like Kitty Wilson, but it wasn't her.

Eamonn withdrew his hand as if from boiling water. 'Ah ha!' he said again and rushed further up the platform to catch the lady in question.

I never did meet the first lady he surprised and I sometimes wonder what she made of it all.

It is true that some people find *This Is Your Life* a little embarrassing at times. The traditional stiff upper lip does not allow many people to touch or hug or show their emotions and this is one of the great problems of the programme. I remember one particular *Life*; the man was a paramedic out in Afghanistan who had driven an ambulance and saved many lives under the most dangerous conditions. He had been invited to our studio to, he thought, watch a programme about the ambulance service. The programme started and Eamonn made his way from the stage to the audience and started to talk to various people seated by the aisle. He worked his way over to the unsuspecting chap and then showed him the Red Book and said the words: 'This Is Your Life.'

Matthew Lethbridge, BEM, was on live television when he calmly looked up at Eamonn. He went throughout the entire programme without any emotion and Eamonn began to worry that we had chosen the wrong type of person. None of his family or long lost friends brought so much as a blink from a face set in stone. It did not feel like a good show. As the cameras were switched off Matthew went over to one of our researchers, clasped her to him and burst into tears. It had been the greatest night of his life he told her.

But fifteen million people at home were convinced he hated it. Sometimes you just can't win!

I suppose it was a little daunting for a girl new in the job of research to be sent out to Los Angeles with the express instructions to film a message from Anthony Quinn for the *Life* we were doing on Ray Milland.

I had emphasised just how important this message was to our story and she left the office with grim determination. I had also hired a freelance American film crew to be at the hotel. They would meet my researcher and do the shoot. As these things happen, Anthony Quinn was himself delayed, and as he had to be off to a location film, he only had fifteen minutes to spare.

The camera crew waited patiently in the hotel reception area but our girl began to wind herself up to a frenzy of nerves, terrified that she was running out of time. Dark thoughts about going six thousand miles back to London without the film message began flitting through her mind when she saw Anthony Quinn coming down the hotel stairs.

She jumped up and realised that her film crew was drinking beer in the bar. With a tight internal scream she leapt off to find them, running at full speed through the entrance to the bar – only it wasn't the entrance, it was an ornate mirrored alcove. I don't know what her exact speed was as she hit the solid glass wall but it was enough to knock her out. She woke up to see Anthony Quinn bending over her.

'Are you OK? We've done the film and you have forty minutes to catch your plane.' He then kissed her cheek and was gone.

One of the first programmes I ever directed was an advertising feature presented by Katie Boyle in 1959. I had met Katie for the first time in 1954 when I had photographed her for *Life* magazine. She was modelling some clothes for a charity. She was standing in the wings wearing a magnificent ball gown, but she was tired so kicked off her shoes. It made a fabulous picture and it was published with the clever caption underneath which simply said, 'The barefoot Contessa'.

The country and I fell in love with her then, so I was particularly happy to have the chance of surprising Katie on *This Is Your Life*, but when my team sat down to plan it, we found she was spending the next few months in Italy. OK, we decided, let's do the surprise in Rome and fly her back to London for the show. We then found out that she was going to a special reception in Rome during the following week.

The difference was that for publicity purposes she was going to get there in an open top carriage.

Perfect! I decided, much to Eamonn's unease, that he would be an Italian traffic policeman, complete with moustache. Katie's route would take her past the Coliseum, and that would be the dramatic moment when Eamonn as the policeman would order her carriage to stop.

That was the plan. Eamonn was duly placed in the centre of the road, a very brave thing to do bearing in mind Italian drivers. Our cameras were hidden from view and her carriage appeared right on time. As it approached I gave a signal to Eamonn to get ready, but just then a whole troop of Japanese students surrounded this policeman and demanded to know the best way into the Coliseum.

Eamonn waved them away only to be joined by some Italian tourists who asked him for some other directions – in Italian, of course. Eamonn was becoming desperate and started to run away from the people who followed him. When Katie saw this chaos with a policeman being pursued by a crowd she told the driver to ignore this crazy policeman's orders.

'Stop!' cried Eamonn.

'Drive on!' shouted Katie.

Eamonn then went up to the carriage holding his hand up to Katie, who let out a torrent of colourful Italian.

The coach driver, now thoroughly confused, drove into the kerb side.

Eamonn whipped off his police cap and moustache and, surrounded by some very confused tourists, brought the Red Book from beneath his tunic to say the words: 'Katie Boyle, This Is Your Life.'

It would be impossible to make a programme like *This Is Your Life* without the trust and affection of the subjects (we never say victims!), the guests and an incredible number of people who bend over backwards to help. Nobody appearing on the programme receives a fee (with the exception of the presenter); this is not to save the programme's budget but is based on the principle that friends and relatives of the subject appear on the show because they like the person concerned.

I remember the time when we invited Kirk Douglas to come on for Chaim Topol. They had made a film together and had become friends. It was impossible for Kirk to leave Hollywood because he was in the middle of filming but he offered to tape a special message from his home. I agreed and was surprised when the next day an American phoned me to say that he was Mr Douglas's publicity agent and he wanted to know what the fee was.

I explained that there was to be no fee. This news was greeted by a long silence.

'You mean you want Mr Douglas to provide his own script and his home and film for you for no remuneration?'

'Yes,' I said, 'that describes it exactly.'

'Well, he's not doing it.'

It was clear that the conversation was at an end, but an hour later my phone went again and it was Kirk Douglas ringing back.

'Did you just hear from my publicity agent?' he asked.

I swallowed hard. 'Er, yes I did,' I answered and waited for the onslaught.

'Well, take no notice, he's an asshole. What time will your crew be able to get here?'

Life is sometimes very sweet.

There are a million things that can go wrong with the making of *This Is Your Life* and doing Spike Milligan's life doubles the chances of disaster.

Spike was due to go to a reunion of old wartime mates at Bexhill so we decided that this would be the perfect place to make the programme and everything was set up. We had to rehearse some of the moves for cameras and it occurred to me that, knowing Spike, he might just decide to come a few hours early if the mood took him and I did not want him to catch us in mid-rehearsal.

I asked one of our researchers to follow him and keep telephoning me to tell me exactly where Spike was throughout the day. It wasn't until the afternoon that I received the call from the researcher informing me that he was in jail and could I explain to the police what it was all about. Apparently Spike had seen our car parked outside his house and then again as the day wore on, so he telephoned the police to ask their help as someone was definitely following him. As it was against the researcher's instinct to say why he was following Spike, he was clapped in a cell.

I spoke to the station officer and told him who we were but not what we were doing, but then I realised we would need their help because if my researcher was in jail, who was following Spike? I decided to tell them all our secrets and asked if they could trace his car. The police put out an alert in two counties to find Spike's car, and he turned up on time to be beautifully harassed by Harry Secombe in a farmer's smock and Peter Sellers wearing a German stormtrooper's helmet and a long black leather coat!

The programme continued to ride the ratings with millions watching it each week and because of the high ratings the promotional value to agents, film companies and publishing houses was enormous. If we featured an actor appearing in a theatrical run, the ticket sales rose after we had gone on air.

George Sewell was having a very successful run in the series called *Special Branch* and as he had such a good life story, we decided it was time to feature him. The programme research was going well, especially when we found his brother who he had not seen in many years, working in South Africa. We brought the brother with his South African wife over for the programme. Although he seemed like a fairly tough character he agreed to go under wraps until the show to keep the secret.

On the day of the programme I was rung up at about six o'clock in the morning to be told that our friend had taken his wife out to a local pub for a quick drink and that someone had been less than complimentary about his wife's accent. He returned the compliment by planting a right hand punch across the offender's jaw, neatly breaking it! The call had come from West Hampstead police station, where he was going to be charged that day with GBH.

There were two problems: first that the press would get the story and blow our surprise in the evening papers, and the second that George's brother would not be available for the programme – or anything else – for some time.

I went straight down to the Hampstead court and although I couldn't explain to the officer in charge, I offered to make my explanation to the magistrate in question. To my surprise the magistrate agreed to let the brother go and even more to my surprise he told me he was a fan of the programme. The charge was dropped and the prisoner was put into my charge on the proviso that he would be on the first plane back to South Africa on the following day.

One of our more 'dangerous' surprises nearly caused the end of Eamonn. It was our Christmas programme and the subject was Eamonn's old friend and *What's My Line?* co-star, David Nixon.

Eamonn wanted to give David a very big surprise and since David was a member of the Magic Circle we arranged for him to unwittingly give a secretly filmed demonstration of a trick involving a small cabinet disappearing inside a medium sized Christmas parcel. It provided the perfect opportunity for us and we involved a close colleague of David's to make sure that Eamonn would emerge from the box.

Eamonn was over six feet tall, but he could just about squeeze into the cabinet. We put Eamonn into the box but

David forgot something that he wanted to get just right and started to look for it. Meanwhile Eamonn was beginning to get claustrophobic. He was in fact suffocating! David eventually opened the box just as Eamonn was about to pass out!

The programmes went on and the time flew by with me hardly noticing that it was now April 1983. The Morris family took off for a holiday in Spain yet nothing had really changed to improve things between Anna and myself. I came back from Spain early while the family stayed on for a few weeks. When Anna did return, she had taken the time to think it all out. It was, of course, the oldest and saddest story in the world.

Anna and I would always get on well together but we could not stay married any longer.

We divorced in 1984, in as friendly a way as was possible and we are still good friends to this day. I know of course that it was all my fault, but it was the lowest point in my life. Perhaps my television obsession ruled out me sharing my life with anybody else.

My friendship with Eamonn and Grainne was still strong and they had taken to Anna with great love and affection. I still remember Eamonn's heartfelt reaction to the news of our divorce.

We were just getting out of my car outside his Chiswick flat when I told him. He looked stunned. He stared at me and, standing in the middle of the street, he burst into tears: he couldn't talk and just waved to me and went inside his flat. He spent over an hour that evening talking with Anna on the telephone, trying to get her to change her mind.

But the marriage was dead and there was no going back.

16 Good Times, Bad Times

I recently read somewhere that the first thing that some men of a certain age do after a divorce, is to buy a red sports car. It was 1984, I was divorced and I had just bought myself a red Mazda RX7.

My daughter was at boarding school in Prior's Field in Godalming, and Gregory was at Charterhouse, also in Godalming. They had both been weekend boarders for many years and they were very happy at school. They saw Anna and myself whenever they came home and since there was still a good relationship between the two of us, they did not feel too bad about the divorce. I bought a flat in Richmond and simply reverted back to my old bachelor routine. I simply dived into my work and did not feel guilty about it this time.

This Is Your Life was going from strength to strength, with fantastic audience ratings. I took time off to go over to Dublin and stay with Eamonn and Grainne and their three grown-up children, Emma, Fergal and Niamh. I had been staying with the family from time to time for many years. I enjoyed the golf at Portmarnock and the Andrews family's great hospitality. While I was there Eamonn and I promised each other that we would plan the next series, but somehow we never quite got around to it. We did decide on one thing, however, and that was that it was time that we took the programme out to Los Angeles and made a few *Lifes* out there.

Back in London I was very pleased to hear that Thames were about to bring back *What's My Line?* and since I was the only one old enough to remember it from the first time round, I was to produce and direct it. I had, of course, photographed the programme many times and I knew the setting and design by heart.

Eamonn was going to chair it again, so I decided not to modernise it with high tech backgrounds and an electronic scoreboard, but instead we were going to follow the old style set and for the score Eamonn would turn over the score cards on a wire ring, as he had always done. I was sure that the nostalgia element would make the programme attractive to those who remembered it from the fifties, and would be a novelty for those who didn't.

The format worked the second time around and the programme was a big success. Once the first series was complete I handed the production over to Maurice Leonard, but I decided to stay on as director. This put a big workload onto Eamonn, which was to prove damaging later on.

I have found that it is usually difficult to present the life of a photographer, mainly because the good ones seem to melt into the background and do not get involved with their subjects. It's therefore difficult to get them on to *This Is Your Life* because nobody really knows anything about them. The one exception to this was, of course, Norman Parkinson, whose wonderful and outrageous photographs attracted so many people, from models to royalty.

To surprise 'Parks' we involved Prince Andrew, who knew the photographer very well. We asked the Prince to get him to a photo gallery at three o'clock on the chosen afternoon. He agreed and brought him in for us to spring our surprise. Prince Andrew told me afterwards that it had been difficult because they had had lunch and the Prince was driving with the three o'clock deadline in mind. He knew that he couldn't bring him early so he was dismayed to find that every traffic light turned to green as soon as they approached, so he started to slow down and stop on the yellow. This amazed Norman because that was not the Prince's usual driving style. The Prince finished his story by saying, 'I couldn't do that again, it's far too nerve-racking.'

Prince Andrew did a great job and he's welcome back any time.

Shortly after that we targeted Jimmy Young's life and decided to invade his morning radio show. The plans were going well and Mrs Thatcher agreed to film a message from Number 10 Downing Street. She made a short video message for me in the main reception lounge and after the 'take', which I was happy with, she asked me whether I thought it was any good.

'The point is,' she said to me, 'could I do it better if you were to shoot it again?'

It is difficult to say to any Prime Minister that you think that they could do it better and even more difficult with Mrs Thatcher looking straight at you!

'If you have the time, Prime Minister, why not try?' I said diplomatically.

She did it again and did get it better. As I was leaving I asked her not to forget that the programme was a secret. The Prime Minister stepped close to me and said with some firmness, 'Don't you worry about me, I can keep a secret!'

I suppose she can in her job! I thought to myself.

Mrs Thatcher did keep our secret but one of the newspapers didn't and Jimmy found out. We never made the programme, but I did enjoy shooting Mrs Thatcher's message.

We succeeded in doing Jim Davidson's life and it was as hilarious as you would imagine. After the show Jim enjoyed the party so much that he decided to continue into the small hours by inviting all his friends into town. His wife Julie did not like the idea and a family 'disagreement' took place. Mrs Davidson found herself being taken home as Jim and the lads took off into the night. On Jim's return the house was locked and a divorce followed soon after. You can't blame the programme, but would they have stayed married if we had not picked on Jim's life?

We had one more *Life* to film in London before setting off for Los Angeles and it was to be the lad himself, Derek Jameson. We decided on a tricky but effective way to surprise him by getting one of his friends to meet him for a late lunch on the day and then take a taxi back to the office through Fleet Street. The taxi was in our pay and was briefed to break down at a certain part of the street. In the meantime Eamonn was dressed as a news vendor on the corner, selling the late edition of the *Evening Standard*. By his side was the headline board which shouted in large black print: 'BIG SURPRISE FOR DEREK JAMESON'. Eamonn was also holding a phoney edition of the *Evening Standard* which said, *Derek Jameson This Is Your Life*. Eamonn, of course, was hidden in a high collared raincoat topped with heavy cap and glasses.

All was going well. Eamonn was in place and I was holding the book out of sight behind him. Yes! There was the taxi and it had stopped; an irate Jameson got out and was heading our way just as a very sweet lady came over and asked Eamonn for an *Evening Standard*, not an unreasonable request, really. Eamonn didn't have a real paper but I did. I offered it to her and she accepted it, giving me a pound. I didn't have any change so I said it would be all right if she just took the paper with my compliments. Derek was almost at our corner.

'No,' she said, and insisted on paying, but then she asked for change.

'Not to worry, madam, please have this copy with our compliments,' I said.

'No, I couldn't take it without paying for it,' she said firmly.

There were only seconds to go now and I had to do the drastic thing. I pushed a paper into her hands and said, 'There you are, madam, now shove off!'

She marched away furious but left Eamonn free to throw the surprise at Derek.

If that lady should by any chance read this, please accept my sincere apologies for being so rude.

After that programme we were almost clear for our trip to Los Angeles. I say 'almost' because there was a surprise anniversary party that Grainne was going to throw for Eamonn with some close friends at the private dining room of Fu Tong, their favourite Chinese restaurant in Kensington. I was pleased to join the select group of about ten people. I can't remember all who were there but Rex Harrison was, with his wife Elizabeth. He is not a man you can easily forget, especially that night when after the main dinner various toasts were being made. Somebody suggested to Rex that he should propose a toast to the Irish. He got up and said with more than a twinkle in his eye something to the effect of, 'Here's to two of my very best friends, Eamonn and Grainne,' and sat down.

'Ah but what about the Irish,' said the voice.

Rex looked blank. 'What about them?' he asked, and continued with his conversation across the table.

'You haven't toasted the Irish,' said the voice.

Rex Harrison's voice took on its full theatrical timbre. 'I'm not going to toast them, just our hosts will do.'

'The Irish,' said the voice.

'No!' shouted Rex and Eamonn, who like all of us at that late hour had had more than two drinks, reached over and grabbed Rex's collar with his left hand and was priming his clenched right hand in a very classic boxing stance.

Grainne caught Eamonn's huge fist and sat him down,

saying quietly, 'I think the evening has peaked. Let's all have another drink and go home.'

I was sitting next to Rex Harrison and it occurred to me that if Eamonn had connected with Rex, the actor would have landed across the other side of Kensington High Street.

Elizabeth Harrison said many years later that Rex had done it all quite deliberately as a ruse to put Eamonn off ever trying to do his life on the programme!

The following day we would have our final production meeting at the Teddington studio before setting off for Los Angeles. Eamonn always had the infuriating habit of being just a little early for all his appointments and I was a little late because of the night before. I tore up to the Teddington studios in my red 'divorce special' Mazda. In a panic I parked quickly and leapt out of the car – only I didn't leap quite as well as I intended and pulled something in my back. I arrived at our meeting doing a very good impression of Groucho Marx.

The fact was I could not straighten up and I went to a physiotherapist who helped but warned me that I would have to go on to a powerful course of tablets to keep the pain off until my back settled down. I agreed and started the course. I slept on a hard board that night and arrived the following morning at the airport walking almost normally.

The flight to LA is about twelve hours and Eamonn and I sat together in first class, wining and dining as one is expected to do. Twelve hours, one film and countless glasses of champagne later, we arrived. I was suddenly beginning to slide out of my tiny mind; the champagne had hit the tablets and they had both started to hit me. I got through the customs and made it into the taxi. 'Beverly Wilshire Hotel,' I gasped and sat back in the seat. All was well until I saw a fast food place at the side of our taxi which had simply 'Fatburger' as its name. I started to turn green and felt very strange. I remember saying to Eamonn, 'Here's my passport and money. I think I'm going to pass out – if I do, just get me up to my room and let me sleep.' Eamonn began to panic and by the time we arrived at the hotel I was not on this planet at all, but I thought I could make it to my room.

I left Eamonn with the taxi, went straight to the reception desk, told them who I was and said that I was very ill and had to go up to my room immediately. They got the message and I followed a maid up to my room to find that it was locked and we couldn't get in. In my swaying state I demanded a room, any room, straight away. She left me, leaning semi-conscious against a wall, but I was still there when she came back and took me to another room.

I went in and collapsed on the bed, knowing no more until the following day. In the meantime Eamonn had panicked and told the team I was dead, or at least very nearly. They rushed up to the room I had originally booked and of course it was empty. Nobody in the hotel could find me because the maid had found another room but had not told anyone of her success. So while the producer slept the sleep of the dead, Eamonn and the entire *This Is Your Life* production team of ten searched the hotel from top to bottom, waiting to find my dead body at every turn.

I eventually returned from the 'dead' and spent the rest of the three weeks as a teetotaller.

The programme was wonderful as we were featuring an idol from my early cinema days, Alice Faye. What a fantastic lady and what a guest list for a film nut such as I . . . Bob and Dolores Hope, Fred MacMurray and his wife June Haver, Caaser Romero, Don Ameche, John Paine, Ruby Keeler and Rudy Vallee.

Rudy Vallee always had a reputation of being a bit of a ladies' man and he was determined to maintain his image by telling Eamonn on the programme that he and Alice had had a romance when she was just starting out as a teenage singer. Alice's husband, Phill Harris, sitting beside Alice, looked up at Rudy and said 'Gee Rudy, I never knew we were related.' This was followed by a short silence broken only by

Eamonn's special laugh that he reserved for moments just like those. Apart from that, the programme was nostalgic for everyone and at one point Phill Harris was in tears. Bob Hope saw this and came out with one of his best one-liners: 'I haven't seen Phill Harris cry since they ran out of Jack Daniels whisky in our club!'

Nobody could follow that, and it was a night to remember, but unfortunately Eamonn had caught a bug in his chest from the smoggy air in LA. Although the programme was finished and we took a few days off, Eamonn could not shake the cold. The journey home made him worse because twelve hours in an aeroplane is not the best thing for a bad chest. It took a long while after we got home but eventually he managed to recuperate. Or at least he seemed to.

We went straight on to *What's My Line* and then finished off the rest of the ten programmes left in the *Life* series for 1985–6.

One of the joys of thinking up the 'pick up' or 'hit' is to devise as fiendish a plan as possible which will be fun and a huge surprise.

Once Ronnie Corbett was in the sights of the programme everyone knew that the 'hit' was going to be tricky to do because Ronnie was so experienced he could spot a phoney situation and a camera a mile away. We knew we had to tread carefully.

Ronnie was appearing on the David Frost programme, which also included a series of fast changing sketches. The sketches featured Ronnie Barker, John Cleese and David himself. A special sketch was written into the programme with Ronnie as a downtrodden wimp who was obsessed by the idea that one day Eamonn Andrews would hide in his tiny house and jump out at him and shout 'Alfred Froggins,' (the name of Ronnie's comedy character) 'This Is Your Life!' and carry him off screaming and kicking to his fate.

The sketch was rehearsed throughout the day with Ronnie

playing the scene with Ronnie Barker. The sketch consisted of 'Alfred Froggins' looking under tables and behind chairs and then finally opening his wardrobe to find Ronnie Barker hidden there, playing Eamonn.

On the live transmission, with a studio audience, the programme started and they went into the sketch, Ronnie playing it with gusto on hearing some good laughs from the audience. The sketch was nearing its end and Ronnie, with a great flourish, shouted, 'OK Eamonn, I know you're in there, come out,' and pulled open the wardrobe doors to reveal not Ronnie Barker but Eamonn Andrews who did predictably say, 'Ronnie Corbett, This Is Your Life.'

Nobody heard any more because there was bedlam from the audience while a stunned Ronnie looked disbelievingly at Ronnie Barker, John Cleese and then David Frost.

'You've done this,' he whispered because he had lost his voice with shock.

They all nodded as Eamonn carried him off.

Richard Branson was not only young but a mystery to most people in 1985 when he had just bought his first plane for his new airline project called 'Virgin'. The unanimous opinion throughout the business world was that this was a ridiculous name for an airline and he and it were doomed to failure. I was advised not to target him. 'He was too young, too brash and had upset too many people' was the word.

I still wanted to do it and Eamonn agreed because Richard Branson was a young man who had already done some extraordinary things. We started our research and found out that he was a practical joker who had a barge on the Thames which he used as an office. We felt strongly that if we surprised him in a normal fashion he just might find it boring, so we thought up something special. The plan was for Eamonn to draw up alongside him in a small boat and board him, pirate style.

Someone then suggested that he should go the whole hog

and dress up like a pirate, complete with a dead parrot on his shoulder. Eamonn immediately began to imitate a very good friend of his, Robert Newton, who had immortalised 'Long John Silver' in *Treasure Island*. 'Ah, Jim Lad, ah.' Eamonn got quite carried away and, much to my amazement, agreed to do it.

Luckily for us it was a nice day on the Thames as Eamonn's boat pulled up alongside Richard Branson's barge. Richard was being 'interviewed' by one of our team as a way of distracting his attention when Eamonn, complete with dead parrot, arrived on the deck and gatecrashed his way into Richard's office.

'Ah, me hearties!' Eamonn called out as he approached Richard, who was totally baffled by Eamonn's outfit but agreed to come quietly as we whisked him away from his barge to the shore and a fast car to our studios at Teddington.

He was convinced that his friends had helped us as a form of revenge for the many practical jokes he had played on them, and he was right.

At about this time Tom Brennand and Roy Bottomley decided to part company. I was forced to choose one of them to continue working on the series and I chose Roy Bottomley. Tom left, very upset, so we had a sad start to the next series, but Eamonn was better and we decided to allow more time for an easier workload this time and return to Los Angeles with a few weeks in hand. The two LA programmes featured Christopher Cazenove and Dudley Moore.

Chevy Chase came on to Dudley's programme and almost immediately tripped over a step on the set and fell heavily. He got a very big laugh but I was worried and stood by with the studio nurse after the programme to see whether he was hurt after such a bad fall.

He looked at me with great patience and said, 'That's what I do, I'm OK!'

Robin Williams also came on Dudley's programme. He

entered, and ignoring Dudley, stared in disbelief at Eamonn's suit. He said that he had never seen anything like it before and asked Eamonn where he got it. 'I know,' he said, 'there's a sale on at K. Mart.'

He got an enormous laugh but Eamonn told me afterwards that he was an inch away from hitting him.

Our *This Is Your Life* with Christopher Cazenove gave me the opportunity to meet up with another one of my idols. Burt Lancaster, who was a friend of Christopher's, had agreed to come along only if he could leave straight away afterwards. After the show I went up to him and thanked him for coming and said that his car was ready. He looked down on me with surprise. 'Why do you want to get rid of me so quickly?' he asked. He stayed and I ended up having a long talk with him.

With our trip to the Hollywood 'tinsel town' over, it was back on the plane for home. The programmes were fine but Eamonn had caught the same chest complaint as before. The LA smog and humidity really attacked his system with a vengeance, but Eamonn ignored all advice and went on to finish *What's My Line?* and made another five *Life* programmes. Yet he was not at all well and his chest infection developed into pleurisy. Fighting that, he lost a lot of weight and began to get much weaker. Even so, he was insisting on making some more programmes while I was arranging to cancel the following two. It was early November 1987 when he became so weak that he agreed to take a few days off and go in to the Cromwell Road Hospital.

As soon as he went in, I cancelled the rest of the year's programmes. I thought that with good treatment and a good recovery he just might be able to think about February.

Eamonn would only see Grainne and me at the hospital. By this stage he had lost so much weight that he did not want anyone else to see him. We sat by his bed on a Tuesday and incredibly, he asked me for a script for the *Life* we were

supposed to be doing on Cliff Morgan the following week. I
told him as gently as I could that I had cancelled the shows
until at least February, by which time he would be fighting
fit. He was as furious as his weak condition would allow. As
we left I promised to return the following Wednesday evening to watch a pre-recorded *Life* go out.

I didn't know at the time but Eamonn called Grainne back
and told her that he wanted to see me alone for a short while
on the following night. He had something that he wanted to
talk to me about in private.

I never knew what he wanted to tell me because Grainne
and I were called back that night at three o'clock in the
morning when Eamonn died.

I had lost the closest and best friend that I had known for
over 30 years.

I still miss him today.

17 *Life* Goes On

E amonn's funeral in Dublin was an extraordinary experience; the whole town seemed to be in mourning for its son. The Irish Prime Minister and many senior politicians were present. I sat with Grainne and the children in the first car in the procession. The police outriders and the crowds of people lining the streets gave the journey an unreal atmosphere, and the following day I was back in London.

The newspapers which had often been so cruel about Eamonn in his lifetime were suddenly contrite. His death and funeral made front page news in most of them.

The memorial service at Westminster Cathedral was a huge event with over three thousand people being present, including ministers from all political parties, a wide range of artists from top stars to unknown actors, writers and broadcasters and many sports people. There were also many ordinary people who had never met him but had lived with his image on television and his voice on their radio for over three decades. I was asked to read one of the prayers and, standing on the lectern looking out over Westminster Cathedral, I lost all my nerves and thought that this was a superb way to say goodbye to him.

Grainne was heartbroken by Eamonn's death, and two years later she, too, was dead.

Back in the world of television, Thames was in turmoil about *This Is Your Life*. Could the series continue? And if so, who could front it? A list of possibles was drawn up but there was only one man whom I thought would be capable of doing it and he was not available. Michael Aspel was under exclusive contract to London Weekend Television. I told the company that they would have to drop the series for at least another year during which time I would try out some unknown names. In that way there would be no comparisons with Eamonn and whoever was eventually chosen would have to make their own reputation from scratch. The newspapers, meanwhile, were busy speculating on who Eamonn's replacement would be, from Esther Rantzen, David Jacobs, Sue Lawley and Noel Edmunds to David Frost, Derek Jameson, Bob Monkhouse and Leslie Crowther.

It was at about this time that John Howard Davies took over as controller of the light entertainment department from Philip Jones. John was very fond of rugby and found himself one Saturday at a match at Twickenham. By sheer chance he bumped into Michael Aspel, who was also a fan of the game.

'What a pity we can't get you for our programme,' said John.

'Not totally impossible,' Michael replied. It would seem that through a series of changes in their programming schedules, LWT could release Michael from his exclusivity.

It was possible and it happened.

Michael Aspel joined Thames in July 1988, just in time to make the next series of *This Is Your Life*, due for transmission by that October. Michael and I had worked together before on other programmes. He did not know the *Life* team but it took only a few meetings before we were all very much at home. There was never the question of 'well, Eamonn would have done it this way' because Michael was his own man with his own very distinctive style, and we were going to do it his way. Yet – as ever – the fun and the problems were just beginning.

One huge problem for Michael was that he was following an already established programme that had been a part of Eamonn Andrews' persona for over 25 years. Michael, who had been the subject of the programme back in 1980, told me that he couldn't hear himself say the words 'This Is Your Life' without it sounding like an impersonation of Eamonn.

He would go off by himself and I could hear him saying the words over and over all with different inflections.

It also did not help to know that the man we were after was a shy man who had told all his friends and family that he would run a mile if ever he saw the Red Book. I must confess now that I did not give Michael this information because being Michael's first one of the series, I didn't think he needed any additional doubts. The person we had our sights on was Phil Collins, world famous and highly protected by his friends and management.

The key was in two things; first I promised that if Phil really objected we would quietly withdraw and go on our merry way, and secondly we would get him into a completely natural situation surrounded by his friends to give Phil the maximum confidence.

The ruse we came up with was a journey across Covent Garden that Phil would have to make to attend a meeting to discuss his new film *Buster*. This was when we could get close without Phil spotting our cameras and Michael, whom he knew quite well.

Covent Garden has many buskers and our plan was for several of Phil's music friends, namely Bob Geldof, Midge Ure, Howard Jones, Mark Brzezicki and Mike Lindup, to be buskers in 'down and out' coats and hats. They would be playing in the open and that alone would distract Phil long enough for Michael to get close, providing Michael could also be disguised. Elaborate make ups were not on for Michael because they take a long time and time is in short supply at our 'hits'.

'I know,' I said to Michael. 'Don't shave for a few days

and with a grey, matted wig and a dirty, old, tattered coat plus an old satchel over your arm for the book, that will give at least twenty seconds by which time you are in business or we'll all go home. Oh, and just for a bit of fun, how about playing an old violin?'

Michael looked at me as though I was completely mad. He is always squeaky clean and the idea of not shaving for three whole days and wearing old clothes for his first show appalled him. Then there was the violin!

I hadn't finished. 'And as he arrives I want you to conduct this million pound set of buskers by shouting out, "OK lads, let's play Vollare".'

I had now gone too far; the outfit plus the indignity of the corniest pop number in the world was too much. Michael began to have grave doubts but persuasion and false confidence on my part eventually did the trick and he agreed to give it a try.

On the day in Covent Garden, we set up the hit. It was 2.30 p.m. and Phil was due any minute. Everyone was in place complete with two 'spotters' on radio links back to me so that I could wave Michael in at the right time. The car arrived at one side of the Covent Garden and Phil got out and began to walk across.

Wait, wait, wait for it . . . now! I waved to Bob Geldof who started to play and waved to Michael who yelled out 'Vollare . . . oh-oh.' Then came musical chaos as Phil spotted Bob and stopped to talk to him. He thought they were filming for something or other. Michael then moved into place. I was watching the picture from a high up camera; I crossed everything I had and looked up at the great TV producer in the sky. Please don't let it go wrong, not on the very first show!

Phil Collins was wary of this strange dirty old man closing in on him. Michael threw down the violin, whipped off his wig and shoved the book into Phil's face.

'This Is Your Life, Phil Collins.' The world stopped and

Michael waited. Phil looked really shocked as Bob, Midge and the boys began to laugh and clap. He looked at Michael and then at the book. 'Oh shit,' he said and smiled and we knew it was going to be all right.

The show was Michael's from that moment on, but that doesn't mean it got any easier. Nigel Mansell was one person we had been trying to get for a long time as he was a rare British hero trying for the elusive world championship (the year was 1988). I wanted to do his story very much but I was concerned by the research coming in which indicated that he was a very reticent and private man. Danny Blanchflower loomed up again in front of me. His wife and close friends were consulted but nobody could predict his reaction to Michael and the Red Book.

Where could we surprise him in such a position that he could not possibly run away? It would seem a good idea to pull the surprise at the end of a race, just as he was getting out of his car, but what would we do if Nigel had just lost the race and was furious with himself and the world in general? No, we could not present our surprise at that time.

The answer came from the research. Nigel loved to fly and was a regular guest pilot with the Red Arrows. Off we went with the camera crew to RAF Scampton, where we spotted him taking off in a Red Arrow supersonic jet.

I had access to the airfield control radio feed so I knew when he would land. It was the perfect set up. With Nigel getting out of the cockpit, he wouldn't have much choice but to accept the Red Book. Nigel taxied his plane around to a standstill and Michael and the cameras were off and running. Nigel released his cockpit canopy and there was Michael waving the Red Book right under his nose.

We need not have worried. Nigel was stunned but he agreed to go on the show. He later told Michael and me that he had two main ambitions left in life. One was to become the world champion and the other was to have a *This Is Your Life* about him. It was an inspiring compliment and I will never forget the moment in the studio when the opening music started and Nigel walked out to see his family on the set – the tears were streaming down his face.

An early mishap nearly finished off one of our other programmes. We were going to surprise Claire Rayner on board the 15.25 train from Huddersfield, with Michael dressed as a ticket collector. We couldn't get on the train as Claire left Huddersfield because she would have spotted us, so we arranged that the camera crew, Michael and I would jump on at Stevenage. Michael and I arrived at Stevenage but we got the message that our camera team had got on the wrong train.

There isn't a lot you can do about that situation except say a few prayers.

The crew arrived with seconds to spare and we all made it on the right train just a few carriages behind a blissfully unaware Claire Rayner. Our lighting man was told that he could plug into the electric circuit of the train, which he did – and all the lights went out. A couple of minutes later the power was restored and we got to about ten yards behind Claire when our main video camera jammed. I pulled Michael back just in time. The train was due in King's Cross within a few minutes, but by the time the camera was fixed we had just two minutes to go. We got her, but it was too close for my liking.

David Shepard the wild life painter was a superb subject for the programme. He just sat back and enjoyed every moment of it but his is the only programme that I have arranged and not been present in the studio to make. A day before the programme was due to be made, I was called to the bedside of my mother.

It was a Saturday in February and my mother, who was 86, had reached her final day. I sat beside her, holding her hand as she slowly slipped into a deeper and deeper sleep. It took over two hours. I watched her breathing getting softer and slower; her hand was that of a small child.

I have often felt as though we are all on a train travelling towards the same destination. We may be in different carriages, but all travelling at the same speed, the young in the carriages farthest from the front. Every time the front carriage with the old or dying finishes its journey, the next carriage takes its place and a new carriage joins at the back. I don't see this as morbid or anything to fear; on the contrary, I really believe that dying is the greatest adventure of all.

My mother died while I held her hand and a split second before she went she opened her eyes. I moved close and around in front of her eyes and kissed her, and then she was gone.

My personal carriage had moved a little further up towards the front.

Michael has a wicked sense of humour which was much in evidence when we were hiding from Sir Cyril Smith who was due to arrive at Rochdale Town Hall. Mandy Lee, our programme organiser, had arranged for Michael to be made up in a nearby hotel. The booking was, of course, made in my name and no one at the hotel knew of our plans. Once at the hotel, Michael, myself and the very attractive make-up girl approached the reception desk. I asked for the key to a room booked in my name and the receptionist gave me the key. She added that it was a single room while staring at Michael, me and the pretty girl who had turned up with a rubber shawl and a small basket full of little camel hair brushes.

'Will you be wanting breakfast?' she asked.

'No,' I replied, 'we're only using it for an hour.'

It was then I began to realise what the receptionist was getting at and I looked at Michael who was staring straight ahead with a very determined look.

When we were in the room and the make-up was finished,

Michael suggested to our make-up girl that she rush downstairs to the reception area sobbing her heart out. I was sorely tempted but thinking about the possible headlines in the local paper the next day I advised against it.

One of our very best *Lifes* was for Billy Marsh, who is an institution in the world of theatre, film and television. He is one of the most respected showbusiness agents and it was for this reason that we broke one of our unwritten rules on the series. We never usually feature producers, agents or managers because it puts the guest artists who appear on the programme in a false light. They are, after all, only connected to that person through business reasons and those are the wrong reasons for the programme, but Billy Marsh was an exception as he is a man who transcends the normal professional relationship with artists.

Our programme included the likes of Bruce Forsyth, Norman Wisdom, Leslie Crowther, Michael Grade, Mike Yarwood and many others. It was a very moving evening. Billy was brought into the studios by his partner Jan Kennedy, expecting to see a studio audition, so he was stunned to see the full audience and cameras waiting for him.

He was reminded of the programme once again a few weeks later when he was presented to the Queen Mother at a special reception. The Queen Mother, who recognised Billy from all the Royal Variety Shows he put on, stopped the procession to ask him how he enjoyed his *This Is Your Life*. After hearing his answer the Queen Mother moved up the line until another thought crossed her mind. She stopped and went back to Billy, causing some small chaos (processions are not designed to go in reverse), to ask him specifically whether he had been surprised by the Red Book.

The protocol involved in addressing dignitaries can sometimes be tricky, but not for Michael. When we were recording Denis Healey's life we had video link-ups with some rather formidable guests. Henry Kissinger, Mr Lee

Kuan Yew, the Prime Minster of Singapore, and Helmut Schmidt, the German Chancellor, all made their formal contributions to the show.

Once the link-up was over Michael turned to the screen and said, 'Thank you, lads.'

Many of the team said we were dicing with death to plan the programme on Oliver Reed. As far as I was concerned he was a wonderful actor, one of the country's most famous, and I felt that the public had taken him to their hearts. Oliver's brother had promised to keep him on the straight and narrow because Ollie's drinking bouts were the stuff of legends. On the day he was as good as gold, we did a wonderful programme at the Royalty Theatre and all Oliver's friends were there. The programme finished at about 7.30 p.m. and we had booked the bar area of the theatre for our private party afterwards. Oliver drank with each of his friends and as the evening wore on things began to warm up, and much alcohol was disappearing, but that was all right with me. Nobody got paid to come on to the programme and therefore it was out duty to see that they were well entertained afterwards. That was fair in my book. The manager of the theatre, however, did not see things quite that way and began to grumble about the rowdiness that was going on.

'I'm going to close the bar,' he informed me.

'No, you can't do that, these are our guests and we have hired the theatre for our programme and the party.'

He was not happy and threatened to call the police.

'Well, I'm not going over to Oliver Reed to tell him and his friends to get out.' I turned to the irate manager. 'You can if you wish.'

'Yes, I will,' he said, and we all winced as he went over to the table and proceeded to have a long conversation with Ollie.

I watched Oliver as his happy expression changed into the sort of evil one that his many screen villains had adopted. He then seemed to rise in slow motion holding the manager in the air. I went over as quickly as I could carrying a crate of beer. 'Here we are, gentlemen, take this with you into your waiting car. Will this be enough?'

Oliver paused, smiled thanks and decided to put the manager down as opposed to throwing him across the room. He and his friends and two crates of beer then went almost quietly into the night and from there I know not where.

I do know, however, that I like Oliver Reed very much.

It's not generally known but Michael is claustrophobic so was not happy when he was asked to surprise Harry Corbett on stage during a performance with Sooty. The difficulty came about because we needed Michael to walk onto the stage without Harry knowing it was him until the very last minute. A full size Sooty outfit was made and Michael was not keen to get into it. It fitted very well but Michael's hands were inside two Sooty paws and he felt that he was trapped inside with no way of getting out.

'Why would you want to get out?' I asked him innocently, but Michael was getting so panicky we had to do something.

In the end we cut off the ends of Sooty's paws and Michael stopped feeling quite so trapped. He did not now want to get out but knew that he could if he really needed to. Please don't ask me to explain the logic of all that, suffice to say that it worked. Michael walked on as Sooty and Harry was well and truly 'teddied'.

The series was going so well that we felt confident enough to go back once again to Los Angeles and this time make three programmes. We used a studio in the middle of Los Angeles where a new set was designed and we were in business. The first programme was to feature Zsa Zsa Gabor. We invaded Zsa Zsa's fantastic house in Beverly Hills with our camera team and then brought her back to our studio. The programme went smoothly with Zsa Zsa's prize-winning race-horse coming on at the end of the show. Unfortunately the horse was very nervous but obviously rather excited in the way that horses sometimes can become. Luckily his impressive condition was avoided by the cameras and all was well.

The next programme was based on Stephanie Beacham's life. She had quite recently established herself in Hollywood as a leading soap queen in *The Colbys*.

She is a smashing lady and was very surprised to see us in the middle of an LA private club where we sprung our surprise.

Our relationship with the press is sometimes contradictory because, on the one hand, they represent a threat in that they can blow a programme if they find out about it before we pull our surprise. The fact that they would destroy a programme for the subject and the viewers is not a factor in their minds when it comes to creating a good front page story.

But, at the same time, our programme likes publicity from time to time. We were in the Universal Pictures Theme Park, Los Angeles, where Michael Aspel was to present the opening of a special *Life* surprise to William Shatner of *Star Trek* fame.

The wonderful thing was that the theme park featured a real life size version of the control deck of the Starship Enterprise. What better place to surprise 'Captain Kirk'. The problem was, our cameras and crew were seen by a reporter working for one of the Hollywood scandal sheets. I knew that he would not be adverse to sending an extra feature or two to the English press for some extra money.

We had invited William Shatner to the *Star Trek* set to have what he thought was an interview for British television. He was due at around 3 p.m. and Michael and I were at the set working out the camera angles. The reporter became suspicious and stood at the back of the set just waiting to see what would happen. Luckily, my son, Gregory, who was 18 at the time, was with us and I persuaded him to sit in at the controls as Captain Kirk. I then began to move the cameras around him with Michael acting out the part of the surprise.

I called the reporter from the back row up to the set and told him that we were from London and that we were shooting some promotion spots with a newly discovered young lad well known on British children's television. I then asked him (from my own early press experience) for what every reporter and photographer hates most in the world. I looked at him earnestly. 'Could you possibly take some publicity stills for use in London and perhaps you could also get them published in Los Angeles?' He was gone so fast he couldn't hear our laughter.

William Shatner arrived soon after and Captain Kirk and Michael Aspel were both 'beamed down' to the studios.

William Shatner's 'Life' was the last of the three programmes in Los Angeles. It was a fast and furious show with Leonard Nimoy aka 'Mr Spock', stealing the limelight.

After the three programmes were finished we could all relax. We did that in grand style at a forties music restaurant called the 'Midnight Tango'. Apart from our director Brian Klein dropping two bottles of champagne over Michael's trousers it all was frantic fun and went on into the small hours.

The strangest incident came outside my work commitment with Michael. By coincidence London Weekend Television were doing a very big award presentation to celebrate the 1990 decade. Lorna Dickinson is Michael's very attractive LWT producer who makes all his *Aspel And Co.* late night chat shows. She had come to Los Angeles on behalf of LWT to set up some presentations. Lorna is a very efficient wheeler dealer and had persuaded ex-President Ronald Reagan to make himself available to be filmed in his own official office accepting an award from the then Prime Minister, Mrs Margaret Thatcher, who would be in London.

The idea was that Michael and Lorna would go to the ex-President's office and make the film on the day before we left for home. I asked Lorna if I could come along just to see the filming and maybe meet Ronald Reagan. She had no objection but pointed out that they had all been cleared by his security department many weeks before, so she couldn't promise I would get in. I had nothing to lose so I went along anyway. Our cab driver, like every one of his colleagues in LA, had just arrived from the Ukraine and had no idea where any place was, got lost and we were late. Lorna had a large carrying case with some camera equipment and I carried it in for her. Amazingly for someone who had not been vetted for security, I was allowed in carrying a case that could have contained several hand grenades. Perhaps I've just got an honest face!

I was about to meet the ex-President of the United States of America, Mr Ronald Reagan, who in his previous movie career I had watched many times in the 'Cally' Mayfair Cinema. I was inside the presidential office; the large desk certainly looked the part with its rich wood and thick leather top. Behind the desk was a column with a huge sculpted Bald Eagle and the inevitable Stars and Stripes on the other side.

It all felt so unreal as I looked out from that 30th floor at the skyline of Los Angeles. Suddenly a door opened and this tall 'Spitting Image' like figure popped out from the door frame.

'Hi, are you ready for me?' the ex-President said.

We begged for just two more minutes to finish off the lighting.

The shoulders shrugged. 'OK. I'll come back,' and he was gone.

The security man was really becoming a pain. He warned us that time was running out. Then Ronald Reagan came in 'I've got this story about Prime Minister Thatcher.' I looked at the security man and raised my eyebrows into an unspoken question . . . time? He remained impassive. The ex-

President went on to tell us about the time that he and Mrs Thatcher attended a summit meeting of all the world leaders at which time she had got their attention and carefully explained to them whenever they got stuck and things got too difficult then they should always leave it to the women to solve it because women were so much better about making decisions than men.

He told the story with plenty of animation; he roared out laughing first and then we joined in.

Time really was running out and Margaret Thatcher was going to give the award to the camera in London and then we would see the ex-President appear to accept it from her. It was felt, however, that someone had to actually hand it into the picture for Mr Reagan to physically take it. Would I stand in for Mrs Thatcher? Would I? Would Madonna like publicity? Would Gazza like a World Cup goal? So, in one magical moment standing with the ex-President of the United States of America in his office, I was representing the Prime Minister of Great Britain, Mrs Margaret Thatcher.

'Action!'

The cameras rolled and Ronald Reagan went to his desk. He looked at me and out of camera on Margaret's behalf I handed him the scroll.

'Thank you, Margaret,' he beamed at me and I actually blushed.

Then the ex-President shook hands, thanked us all and left. In moments I was back in the real world sitting in a Lithuanian driven taxi, wondering if all that had really happened.

We were now almost finished in Los Angeles but Michael had one more award presentation to do. The award was going to Michael Jackson and, having heard such strange and wonderful things about the singer, I decided to go along just for the fun of it.

Although the handing over of the award was supposed to

have been arranged, there was nobody waiting for us as we arrived at his secret house in Santa Monica. The front looked like a derelict warehouse with graffiti over the metal shutters.

We waited and would have given up except that Michael (Aspel) spotted a small camera with a button underneath it. We pressed it and looked up at the unblinking eye.

A metallic voice suddenly said, 'Yeah?'

We introduced ourselves and explained the purpose of our visit to the distant voice who had yet to admit that this was where Michael Jackson lived. A click and the shutter opened and we went into a small courtyard with trees and a small path, but there was still nobody to be seen and nobody came to meet us. This was more intriguing than insulting so we decided to explore until we came to another wall and a door which was locked and barred, but with another electronic eye gazing down from above the door. We repeated our names and the reason for our visit all over again, and the door opened.

Inside was a small room with nobody around so we stayed a while and then a huge bodyguard came towards us.

'Y'frm iglind?' I think he said. Michael was getting annoyed.

He asked us to wait and then left. 'That was fairly polite,' I said to Michael. The giant came back and without saying a word, pointed to another door.

Michael and I looked at each other like Abbott and Costello – I felt like Costello and Michael was beginning to look like Abbott. We went into the room which was lit like a tiny film studio with a piano in the background. The place looked empty until we saw that standing near the piano was a tiny figure with his back to us. He turned but would not walk out of the spotlight that was pointed at him, so we went over towards him.

'Hello,' he whispered. Michael and I strained our ears to hear him.

'Hello,' we said in response but he still didn't move.

Michael explained why we were there and that he had brought him a present from England.

We witnessed a transformation; he actually moved closer to us and became excited at the thought of a present.

Michael gave him a tin of special tea from Piccadilly. 'It's called Jackson's Tea,' he said.

The multi-billionaire was absolutely thrilled with this and kept turning it over in his hand. Quite forgetting his so-called problems about touching people, on my introduction I offered my hand to him, immediately thinking how stupid I was, but he took my hand and shook it just like a normal human being. In fact he turned out to be an extremely nice person. Michael presented him with the award which was recorded on Michael Jackson's own television camera and he then handed the tape cassette to my Michael to take back to LWT in London. I asked if I could take a photograph of the two of them together. Michael Jackson agreed and I took a picture that eventually ended up in *Hello!* magazine.

We said our goodbyes and he thanked Michael once again for the tea and moved back into the spotlight. We reversed the route through the security maze and were soon back in the street and the real world. Luckily our car was still there with its wheels still on, the driver was still there too, and we made it back to our hotel and a very real gin and tonic. It had been a very strange day.

We were back in London the following day and busy preparing our American programmes for transmission during the Christmas period. There was no doubt now that the programme fitted Michael like a glove and he had made it his own. In many ways he brought the programme into the nineties.

We kicked off the new decade by doing the life of one of Britain's best-loved comedians. You can be sure that anything to do with Ken Dodd is going to be unusual. He does not live on the same planet as most of us; instead he is on permanent tour around the country, or 'Doddyland' as he calls it. His ambition is to play every theatre in the country and he must be pretty close to achieving his aim. This time he was booked into the London Palladium for six weeks, so we knew where he was going to be.

Monday 19 February 1990 was the day. Ken was due to attend his first rehearsal at the theatre with the musicians and dancers. The plan was for Michael to hide on stage until the rehearsal was over and then appear out of a suitable piece of scenery. We expected this to be around five o'clock that afternoon and our studio was all set for the actual programme at seven. Annie, who had been with Ken for many years and looked after all his arrangements, was, of course, in on the secret. I kept in close contact with her and knew they were staying at a small hotel in Kensington.

On that Monday I was going over all the last details with the associate producer Johnny Graham when a pale-looking researcher came into my office waving a newspaper.

'It's all off,' she said.

John and I looked at each other. 'Is he dead?' we both asked at the same time.

She showed us the front page of *Today* newspaper whose headline read 'Ken Dodd: This Is Your Life'. The article went on to say that we were planning to do Ken's life that evening and that he knew all about it. I immediately phoned the hotel and got through to a puzzled Annie. 'No, he definitely does not know,' she told me.

'But he will as soon as he reads his morning paper or somebody phones him to talk about it,' I said. Annie went on to tell me that Ken, like most theatre people, was not an early riser. We then went into action. 'Right, keep him in bed and get the hotel to stop all his incoming calls.' Annie had a slight smile in her voice when she said that stopping his calls was easy but how did she keep him in bed?

'Oh, you'll think of something.' I then went on to tell her

that all she had to do was to make sure he went straight to the Palladium after he had woken up.

'But once he's there everybody will be talking to him,' she said.

'Don't worry, we will surprise him as he arrives at eleven o'clock and do the show at two.'

A muted cry went up from Mandy Lee, the programme organiser, who demanded to know how we were going to bring every invitation and all our arrangements forward by five hours. I couldn't answer because I had already left to explain to the director that he had the same problem.

All that remained now was to change the rehearsal by rebooking the musicians and dancers and stage crew.

Ken did have a happy morning in bed, he did not see a newspaper until after our show and he received no phone calls. Our programme was a surprise – except he did say that he'd been expecting us . . . for many years. What had kept us so long? was his question. It was a great show.

Gary Glitter was going to be our next subject and what better place to pull off our surprise than on stage at the end of one of his rock concerts.

A fully packed Wembley Arena has to be seen to be believed. 10,000 excited bodies reaching their own personal climax during a humid two-and-a-half hour rock session has a uniqueness of its own. Gary was just finishing his finale. I was in position standing in the well between the audience and the front of the stage and Michael was backstage. Timing was to be everything.

The noise was deafening as Gary took his bow and then Michael, complete with Red Book under his arm, walked on to the stage behind Gary. Even Gary was surprised at the extra roar from thousands of hoarse throats. The audience could see what Gary couldn't – Michael was moving up behind him. The sound began to take on a physical proportion. Gary saw Michael and jumped up in the air with shock, then ran around the stage shaking his head in disbelief. Yes, I thought, we have him, and then the crowd began to get hysterical.

I stood in front of the stage looking up from the narrow well trying to judge which one of the hand-held cameras would have the best shots when the whole body of the audience standing on that Wembley floor began to move forward against the metal rail. Thousands of people were moving towards me with only that rail to stop them. I could hear nothing but one gigantic scream as unbelievably the rail began to bend inwards.

Frozen by fear I felt that I was facing the collapse of a huge dam.

Gary sensed the danger, stopped still and held one hand up, and the crowd, as if by magic, paused in their pursuit of my annihilation for one second, which was enough time for me to remove myself with Olympic speed from that death-trap.

I heard Michael say, 'Gary Glitter, This Is Your Life' as I ran for mine.

Gary came offstage and shook Michael's hand then said, 'No way.' Had I defied death for nothing?

Michael backed off and Johnny Graham put his arm around the departing Gary. 'What's wrong?' he asked him.

Gary told Johnny that he couldn't do the show because he would miss his mother who was alive but too old to make it to the studio. Gary was told that his mother knew all about the programme and would be upset if it were not to happen.

We made the show. Gary's mum was next to him and stayed for the party afterwards which finished at about four in the morning.

There could be no greater contrast than that between Gary Glitter's Wembley concert and 10 Downing Street. Unfortunately, Downing Street was being redecorated, so when Prime Minister John Major agreed to film a message for *This*

Is Your Life I had to shoot it at a very luxurious room at Admiralty House. Not quite Downing Street, I know, but the contrast is still there. Mr Major is a great cricket fan and was especially fond of the famous cricket umpire Dickie Bird.

I had been advised that Dickie was a very shy man indeed and would not take kindly to the programme. Others advised for it and we decided to chance it. The Prime Minister's message would be the icing on the cake. Waiting for the Prime Minister reminded me of when I filmed Mrs Thatcher, who had insisted on filming her spot again because she thought she could do it better.

Mr Major arrived and expressed to me his admiration of Dickie Bird. I was at a loss because I know nothing of cricket and was reluctant to tell the P.M. of my one-game school cricket career. We therefore had very little to discuss other than how I was going to film him and where. 'How long do you want?' he asked me, and I said two minutes or so would be fine.

Mr Major was excellent. He delivered a moving message into the camera and I was delighted. Then he surprised me by saying exactly what Mrs Thatcher had said.

'I think I'd like to do it again. I can do it better,' and he did.

What is it they say about great minds?

Joseph Locke has had a legendary life and like all good legends, fact and fiction are very hard to separate. Faced with the Red Book I was convinced he would say 'no' because he would not wish the 'legend' to be examined too closely. He had been away from day-to-day performing for many years until he acquired a whole new audience following the release of a film loosely based on his life called *Hear My Song*, which seemed to us to be the best topical peg to hang the story on.

We then became a little devious, knowing that Princess

Diana was attending the special charity film night and so we advised the royal press office of what we were going to do. We got the 'go ahead' from them and I knew then that if Princess Diana was in on the secret there was no way that Joseph could walk away.

Michael leapt onto the stage after the film just as Joseph was ending his speech. Showing the Red Book to Joseph he held his breath.

Would he or wouldn't he?

Joseph looked at Michael and then at the Princess in the theatre.

'Did you know about this?' he asked her. The audience laughed and so did the nodding Princess.

He turned to Michael and gave him a twinkling smile as if to say, 'I know I've been stitched up.'

It was a nostalgic programme and nobody from the Inland Revenue – which had been chasing Joseph for many years – was invited.

The Winter Garden Theatre at Blackpool is a wonderful place with an exciting atmosphere and in September 1993 Little and Large were appearing for the season. What better way to kick off the new series of *This Is Your Life* than with the lives of those two, we thought. We decided that Michael would surprise them both on stage and then whisk them away by car to the Granada studios in Manchester, where we would do the programme.

At this time I was directing what we call the 'hit' or the 'pick up', which is in fact the surprise at the beginning of the programme. These are tricky unrehearsed moments which have to be directed by the seat of my pants.

That night I had planned a spectacular opening. Michael would be standing in the centre of Blackpool with me shooting him from the very top of the Blackpool tower. It seemed a good idea at the time but I had not counted on feeling sick from the top of the tower and I had not counted on just how difficult it was going to be to shoot Michael from a quarter of a mile away on a telescopic lens.

It was dark and Michael was ready in the high street, so I gave the signal for Michael to start his walk along the street talking to the tower at a camera he couldn't see. All was going well until a police car began to circle this man walking along holding a red book and talking at the moon. They eventually stopped him in the middle of our 'take' and, even though they recognised him without any cameras present, decided to investigate further. Michael managed to persuade them that there really was a camera at the top of the tower and all was well . . . Except it wasn't, because when we went over to the theatre to invade the stage we found that Little and Large were doing a 'Singing in the Rain' routine with a few thousand gallons of water being poured all over the stage and them. Now all that is fine until you decide to take high voltage television cameras and sound cables and live microphones into the deluge.

Two umbrellas and a see-through plastic rainsheet later, Michael went forth.

I closed my eyes waiting for the sparks, which miraculously did not come. Later a colleague pointed out to me that we were not insured for Michael's electrocution. I made a mental note to get that seen to back in London – and, oh yes, the programme went very well.

The rumours I had been hearing on and off for the past four years had turned out to be true and the BBC were indeed in secret talks with Thames about buying *This Is Your Life*. They wanted the programme they had rejected in 1964 as played out and finished. Now, 30 years later, having been thoroughly beaten in the ratings for 25 years on a Wednesday night, the BBC decided 'if you can't beat them, buy them', and that's what happened in 1994.

The deal was for Thames and its team to make the programme for the BBC. Once the initial excitement was over a whole lot of new problems surfaced: should the programme be changed, should it be different?

Peter Estall was the executive producer for the BBC and his was the unenviable task of liaising between me and the team and his own departmental requirements. A bigger set, more expensive opening titles and new musical arrangements all helped give a wonderful, fresher look to the programme.

Yet some questions remained unanswered: Who are you going to do? How are you going to do it? And when?

We did, in fact, start with a spectacular programme complete with a 30-piece orchestra conducted by Michael Reed to provide the music for the life of Sir Andrew Lloyd Webber. The surprise was sprung at the Adelphi Theatre during the opening of Andrew's *Sunset Boulevard*. Elaine Paige, Paul Nicholas, Glenn Close, David Essex and Michael Ball all sang live with the orchestra for Sir Andrew, but the big problem was whether to ask Sarah Brightman to be on the show. Her divorce from Sir Andrew wasn't that long ago but she wanted to be present.

Sarah sang beautifully for him and they embraced at the end.

But the Sir Andrew Lloyd Webber *Life* had another drama attached to it that would have done any film script proud. Elaine Paige was delighted to be asked to appear as a guest of Sir Andrew because of the many shows they had made together which had, in turn, made Elaine the star she is today.

Two months before our invitation Elaine was working so hard that her voice gave out and she had the nightmare that all singers dread, trouble with her throat. Her vocal cords were strained and she was told not to sing for a few months to allow her throat to recover.

Elaine was convinced she could not sing to the quality that would be needed for an occasion that big, live for television with a 30-piece orchestra in front of everybody in show business. It was a formidable undertaking at any time but with doubtful vocal cords she was terrified. We agreed to have her on the show for just a message and a hug for Andrew. With two weeks to go it began to haunt her. She phoned John Graham (my associate producer and all round genius) and told him that she just had to sing.

'I'm not going to miss this magic event with everybody singing but me.' But her fear was still there.

I made sure that she understood that we were not putting any pressure on her to do this. It could go disastrously wrong and ruin her voice and her career. The night of the show arrived, we started the programme and when her turn came she ran onto her mark in front of the orchestra and the introduction started. Elaine stared ahead and quickly swallowed, drawing a breath. I found myself standing behind the main camera clenching my hands into tight fists. Then Elaine started to sing her famous number *Memories* from *Cats*.

She was a stunning success and when she finished she smiled with her tears and clasped Andrew to her. He thought she had never sounded better and on the strength of that night, decided that she should take over the lead role in his West End production of *Sunset Boulevard*. A wonderful and very dramatic evening which started the first of our new series of *This Is Your Life* for BBC Television, Wednesday, 2 November 1994.

With most television programmes the producer's job, no matter how difficult, is clear cut. You get the production on the air to the best quality you can and within budget.

This Is Your Life, however, has a very rare and strange quality which means that it cannot abide by the usual rules. For example, nobody realises that after a recording of the programme I am committed to the wishes of the subject and not Thames Television or the BBC. If the subject were to ask me not to transmit the programme for a good reason, then I would accept the request and the programme would not be broadcast.

To the best of my knowledge, no other television programme is made on that basis. It is a very expensive production and cancellation would cost everyone a great deal of money, but there would be no doubt in my mind. It would still not go out. There are two secrets within the programme. One is that I would not go ahead with the surprise if I knew for certain that the subject knew about it. The other is that even after we have made the programme, we do not tell the audience at home who the subject is to be on that transmission night.

Sometimes a newspaper finds out who it is to be transmitted on a specific date. When this happens and it is accurate, I simply change the scheduled programme for another recording. I have warned various newspapers that I will make this transmission change even within one hour of it being broadcast. In that way it is impossible for them to get it right, unless they can issue a new edition less than 60 minutes before our transmission at 7 p.m.

There is another self imposed rule that, apart from two exceptions (Eamonn Andrews and Lord Louis Mountbatten), a transmitted programme is not available for rebroadcast in the event of a famous celebrity dying. When any famous person dies suddenly then there is always a terrible rush from all the television companies to put something on the air as a tribute to them.

What better way, it seems to them, than run a recent *This Is Your Life* and their problem is solved. The requests come in from all the news departments of ITN and the BBC and now all the others. The requests always start off urgent and then become demanding. My refusal does not make me popular amongst the news companies – including the news department of Thames when it was broadcasting.

The reason for my negative reaction is not simply a sense of respect for the departed, but because of a deeper understanding of the nature of the *Life*. The programme is an accolade in the form of a party to celebrate someone's life and sometimes the person we feature is quite old. How would you feel if you were appearing on your own obituary? It would become very depressing for the subject, who could quite understandably think well that's that, the only thing left now is for me to die. That's not what *This Is Your Life* is about. It's not going to become a death song for anyone feeling a bit under the weather or over 'three score years' or more.

Should we do Sir Peter Ustinov? was the debate at the programme meeting. We had done his life before but that had been back in 1977, over seventeen years ago, another lifetime ago, in fact. But where was he? That was to be the biggest problem, according to his wife and family. When he was not working he just took off and nobody was really quite sure where.

We fixed a date for when he was next due in London for a tour, but a few days before our programme date he vanished from home, saying that he would see them all in a few days' time. I knew that he was a highly regarded member of UNESCO so we contacted a few of his friends there. Paris ... he's in Paris, we were told. OK, we'll go to Paris, I thought.

All the arrangements were made. Michael, myself, Johnny and a camera team were set to find him in Paris when we heard the news that he'd left Paris and was on his way back to Geneva, but not to stay.

'Now hold on,' I said, 'we cannot do a programme on this basis. We'll have to lock him into an important appointment to be sure of his location.' I didn't mind where it was just so long as we knew he'd be there when we turned up. Amazingly, the United Nations came to our aid, telling us they would set up a special press lunch for UNESCO at their headquarters in Geneva and Peter, as a guest of honour, would be there without fail. Our biggest problem would be getting into the UN building because of their massive security.

We were all photographed and security screened but we still couldn't tell security of our true intentions, so we faked a documentary on the spot and began filming all over their site until we got near to the lunch and then one of Peter's friends got us into the dining room.

Peter was making a speech at the end of which Michael and camera crew gatecrashed the room and went up to Peter in front of the world press. Michael flashed the book, which amazed Peter and baffled a few reporters from China.

'What, right now?' Peter looked at Michael who nodded.

Then we were off to Geneva airport and in London on time. One hour later at seven o'clock Peter Ustinov and Michael Aspel were doing *This Is Your Life*.

The next challenge was nearly ruined by myself and my idiot obsessions. The Science Museum in London seemed to me to be the perfect place to capture Arthur C. Clarke, the wonderful author of *2001* and *2010* and many other books of fact and fiction. I love science fiction and was glued to all the Apollo NASA programmes, so when I got the chance to do the programme on Arthur C. Clarke it was my opportunity to dream up the scheme of my lifetime.

Arthur had forecast the use of space satellites for intercontinental communications way back in the fifties, and he had close contact with NASA. One of his closest friends was Buzz Aldrin, the second man after Neil Armstrong to actually walk on the moon.

Buzz agreed to come over and I shook the hand of the man who walked on the moon. I was in heaven.

Arthur was due to arrive at the Science Museum at three o'clock in the afternoon and I had hidden all my cameras and Michael behind the rockets and satellites. As Arthur approached the life-sized mock-up of the moon module, Buzz Aldrin was to step out from underneath the module and be Arthur's first surprise. The module stood on a very convincing landscape – or rather moonscape – and I had received special permission from the Science Museum security for us to cross the barriers protecting this exhibit.

I gave Buzz Aldrin the memo I received from the Museum. It reads: 'This is to give special permission to Mr Buzz Aldrin to walk on the moon surface.'

It was 25 years late but I'm sure he appreciated it.

Just before three o'clock I checked all our final plans as I stood by the Apollo 11 module. I could see and touch the scars on its side from the re-entry back to Earth. This was the stuff that dreams are made of. I couldn't resist the urge to abuse my special museum pass and cross the barrier and climb inside, which I did. It was amazingly small with very little room to move around in. I ran my hands over the instruments that had made history, so it was an abrupt jolt back to earth as someone whispered urgently, 'Get out fast! . . . Arthur's early!'

The trouble was I couldn't get out fast because not having been trained by NASA I did not know the trick and I just fumbled around inside, unable to move backwards. It may have been just 'one small step for man' but it was a giant leap for Malcolm Morris! I was actually so late that the camera was already on when I ran quietly past Arthur C. Clarke as he approached the module. If anyone watches that programme again I'm briefly visible behind Arthur as he met Buzz Aldrin.

Michael made his introductions and Arthur stepped back with surprise, but he proved to be a wonderful subject for a most unusual programme.

Doing *This Is Your Life* in America is exciting and a lot of fun but it's also a nightmare of organisation and very risky because you just don't know what is going to happen until you get there.

As the producer I'm responsible for the budget and the idea of spending many thousands of pounds and coming back to London without a programme is not one I relish. Then why go? Aren't there enough people in this country?

Good questions, but the fact is that with a series of 26 programmes it is important occasionally to have a change of scene. We would do more programmes inside Europe, but the main problem there is language. Like it or not, the country with the same language and the most people that are well known in Britain is America.

The most difficult thing with big American names is getting in contact with the families – wives, husbands and children. Usually the only way is through an agent and because we do not pay any fees, there is nothing in it for the agent but problems if things go wrong.

We do not tell any celebrity what we are doing and if they find out then we are forced to cancel the programme. Therefore it is no picnic getting to the right person. I am spoilt in this country because I can pick up the phone to most agents and managers and get all the cooperation I need.

We have been making programmes in America since 1987 so gradually we are becoming better known over there, but making contact was still the main problem in trying to reach Howard Keel. For years we had made approaches to his Hollywood management without success, but then I got lucky. Planning the *Life* on Sir Andrew Lloyd Webber I went to see *Sunset Boulevard*. Watching the show from my stall seat I suddenly realised I was sitting next to Mr and Mrs Howard Keel. I waited until the interval and then Howard Keel got up to go to the toilet. God bless his bladder, I said to myself.

I said hello to Mrs Judy Keel and luckily for me, she knew of the programme.

I looked around and saw Howard returning so without any more ado I asked her directly: 'I want to do Howard's life in Hollywood; can I call you?'

'Great idea,' she said and gave me her card. That simple approach cut across three years of phone calls to America.

We fell silent as Howard arrived but she did give me a huge wink as they left at the end of the show.

We went over to Los Angeles in January 1995, to be told that he was spending a few days at his home in Palm Springs playing golf. There was no choice but to follow so we flew the team and cameras off to Palm Springs and laid our trap behind the eighteenth hole.

Howard Keel has been a world star for many years and he was bemused and amused by the sheer audacity of an English programme coming over to America to do his life. He agreed and the guest list was amazing; for no payment we got George Kennedy, Linda Grey and most of the cast of *Dallas*, and Jane Powell, Katherine Grayson, Russ Tamblyn and George C. Scott were among the special arrivals, so it was quite a night. It was also remarkable because Howard made a speech to the studio audience at the end of the programme saying that he felt that it had been one of the most memorable occasions of his life.

Judy Keel said to me at the party afterwards how pleased she was that Howard had chosen to go to the lavatory when we met in London!

It would be nice if all my plans were to go so well but I was plagued with problems when we decided to push our luck and go for another world star. The lady in question had been a superstar of the big screen for many years; she had appeared in films with Gene Kelly, Fred Astaire, Gregory Peck, Jane Russell, Danny Kaye, Donald O'Connor and Frank Sinatra. She had done it all – and she was still doing it all at her own hotel in Las Vegas.

It was a great scoop for us when we contacted her son who agreed we could do a programme on his mother, but our troubles setting up a *Life* on Debbie Reynolds were only just beginning.

Firstly, there was no television studio in Las Vegas big enough for our set, so we asked our CBS TV friends Pat Walker and Tom Onge to bring out their own crew to Las Vegas with one of their mobile outside broadcast units and pull the surprise at the end of Debbie's cabaret at the hotel.

After the surprise we would, with her permission, shut her in her dressing room for an hour while we built a new set from scratch with its own lighting and cameras and would invite the existing audience to stay on and watch our programme. All our guests were secretly flown in to Las Vegas and hidden in other hotels along the Strip.

I had been to Las Vegas some years before and as an opener I planned to film Michael in the heart of the town to set the scene for our audience at home. The problem was I would have very little time to shoot. We had to film the opening and within 30 minutes rush to the hotel and hide Michael so that he could walk onto Debbie's stage for the surprise.

No problem. I knew I wanted to film Michael down the Golden Nugget Strip, a vast road of fantastically lit gambling casinos. Our film vans pulled into the main Las Vegas street, only to be stopped by huge barriers across the road. The whole mile and a half of the strip was being redeveloped and it was no longer possible to enter it for the next six months.

I had no time for tears, however, and I spotted another road which would have to do. Michael was busy learning his words and I sent the camera crew off to fix the camera and some lights for the shoot.

Take one: Action! Michael started to walk along the street towards the camera. 'Here we are in Las ...' He didn't get any further as a rather tall policeman on a horse came over and politely asked me what I was doing. Hearing my explanation and my accent he said that it was OK.

'Stand by ...' I said.

'But,' he interrupted, 'where is your pass for street filming?'

'Ah ... ah yes,' I said, 'well, that's been arranged through my location manager.'

My American cameraman looked puzzled. What location manager?

I was now sweating gently. 'Yes, it must be at the hotel with him.' The discussion went on between me and the policeman. The clock was ticking and I began to panic.

'Well,' he said with the sort of finality that policemen deliver.

'Wait,' I said, 'I'm doing this for British television.' He looked very unimpressed. 'For . . . er . . . Thames Television.' He looked blank. 'You know, Thames Television, the people who made *The Benny Hill Show*.'

The world changed, the policeman got off his horse and we discussed Benny Hill for ten minutes, then he rode off saying that I should get on with what I was doing before he came back.

That was good enough for me: Stand by and action, cue Michael. The camera panned to Michael who started walking along the street again.

'Here we are in Las . . .' A car pulled up alongside Michael and three well-wined and dined holiday Brits leaned out of their windows shouting, 'Hello Michael, where's your Red Book? Are you going to do us?'

Stand by for take three. Action! Camera on Michael once more. 'Here we are in Las Vegas . . .'

The cameraman waved his hand in front of the camera. 'Sorry, buddy, our batteries are dead, no problem though, we'll get some new ones from the van, take ten minutes at most.'

Ten minutes later Michael was doing his walk again. 'Here we are in Las Vegas and . . .' Michael stopped. 'And I can't remember the next xxxxxxx word!'

I couldn't blame him. I looked at my watch; we were 30 minutes behind time.

Take five action! This time we got it right, the camera and lights were all shoved back in our van and we went back to the hotel. Michael went off to change his shirt and I went up to my room to collect my other notes. A quick shower and I'd calmed down again. I got into the lift and went down to the show floor – only the lift didn't open and I was stuck inside.

I had disobeyed a cardinal rule of television which is never go into a lift before the making of a programme because you will get stuck. It didn't matter that I had never been stuck in a lift before in my life; if it was going to happen then this would be the time, and it was.

I had always wondered what would happen when you picked up one of those phones in a lift. Well, now I knew. Nothing.

I can panic, I thought, nobody would blame me, I deserve a good panic and a cry, but I really had no time to indulge myself. I pressed both alarm buttons and jiggled the phone at the same time. Eventually an American voice asked me what I wanted and I explained in my best British accent about my predicament. I hope I don't have to get into Benny Hill again, I thought, but the door really was stuck and they had to get their own fireman to attack the outer layer of their door before he got to mine about one hour later.

We eventually made the programme and I got to meet the dream lady of my youth, Miss Jane Russell. Knowing that she was going to be on the show I had come prepared with an original photo of her as she appeared in her first film, *The Outlaw*, lounging back in a hayloft looking sultry. She still looked stunning and I asked her to write something naughty across the photo.

'Like what?' she asked.

'It was a magnificent evening, you were wonderful, love Jane Russell.'

She looked at me and smiled. 'No way,' she said and wrote her best wishes.

But you can't blame a feller for trying.

Spike Milligan, like Peter Ustinov, is someone who we have featured twice on the show. It had been difficult the first time around and nothing had changed. We did not know what his movements were going to be because neither did he.

Spike is a person who will follow his mood as it suits him. The main stabilising influence in his professional life is Norma Farnes, who has managed him for over twenty years. She was the person I got in touch with. Yes, she confirmed, she had booked Spike for a television appearance on BBC's Pebble Mill, near Birmingham. Not only that, but she was going up there with him so that he could be monitored. With Spike you never knew how he would return to London. Would it be by train, plane, hired car or coach party – anything could happen as his mood dictated, but with Norma there we knew that they would be coming back by train to Euston at 1.30 p.m. on 24 January 1995. A meeting was instantly set up with the Euston Station security office and with their liaison we arranged for our cameras and Michael to be hidden in a first floor balcony.

Now only two questions remained. First, which platform would he arrive at and second, how could we distract his attention while Michael ran up to him?

Spike is still very sharp and can also move fast when he chooses.

We decided to tackle the problem in two ways. First, a station announcement would say: 'Would Mr Spike Milligan please look at a message on the central notice board.' Second, the main notice board, which is controlled by a central computer, would be reprogrammed to go blank on all train information and then spell out the words: SPIKE MILLIGAN THIS IS YOUR LIFE. CONGRATULATIONS FROM BRITISH RAIL.

Various people were placed around the station waiting for my signal. I spotted him with Norma and gave the go-ahead to my station friend who spoke to the computer room on his mobile. Another signal cued the station announcer who then made the announcement just as the computer came to life and sent the sign across the board.

Travellers were puzzled as to what was going on and Michael got to Spike as he looked at Norma in amazement.

Before Norma had time to reply Spike saw the book. 'But I've just done a television show in Birmingham and anyway, everyone thinks I'm dead.'

'Oh no you're not,' said Michael. 'Off we go to the studio.'

Spike reacted with a smile and a moan. 'It was done twenty years ago, everybody I know is dead.'

That proved to be inaccurate as the programme, which was scheduled to run to half an hour, ended up by being a one hour special . . . a classic in fact.

Dame Alicia Markova was known throughout the world as one of the greatest ballerinas of all time. We were to spring our surprise on the great lady in the very plush Crush Bar of the Covent Garden Opera House, the scene of many of her ballet triumphs.

She thought she was going to be interviewed for her forthcoming biography *Markova: the Legend*. Although the book was real the interview wasn't but the author, Maurice Leonard, an old friend of mine, had agreed to pretend to be the interviewer.

The plan was that many of her friends, including the dancer Wayne Sleep, were to be hidden behind a panel where the interview was due to take place. On my signal Michael would sneak out from behind the panel on one side while her friends came round from the other; it seemed simple enough to me but everyone else thought this was too dangerous as she might wander round behind the panel when she arrived.

'Why on earth would she do that?' I argued. 'No, don't worry, I'll see the lady goes straight in front of the panel and sits down.'

I was confident I could manoeuvre her to sit in front of it and that was that. Why do people always want to argue with the producer?

Dame Alicia knew that the interview was to be for television, so the cameras would not be a surprise, and I was to be the freelance television director hired for the occasion. Dame Alicia arrived and I graciously greeted her and led her to the chairs in front of the panel as planned.

'Not yet,' she said as she saw a mirror behind the panel and began to move towards it. 'I will just check my hair before we start,' she said quite reasonably.

'You look absolutely wonderful and your hair is perfect.' I led her again towards the chair.

'Thank you, you are kind,' said Dame Alicia, 'but I would like to see for myself,' and once again she pulled her arm out of my clutches and went towards the back of the panel.

I literally jumped in front of her, rudely blocking her way, and I think she was taken aback by my abruptness. 'You can't go in there,' I said as her eyebrows rose. I quickly continued, 'The carpet has just been dry cleaned and is still wet.' I bravely ploughed on: 'And . . . and . . . and it's the chemicals, yes it's certainly the chemicals, oh, I've been warned by the staff that it will rot your shoes, yes, rot them.'

Her mouth began to drop open as I guided her once again back to the seat. I continued with some desperation, 'And I have a large make-up mirror for you.' I had lied, of course, and as she sat down I called out, 'Who has taken the mirror?' I looked around. 'Don't worry, Dame Alicia, it will be here in one moment, and while we wait, would you like a rehearsal?'

She agreed, and as we started her friends came around the panel and Michael arrived on time to take her hand and say the words: 'Dame Alicia Markova, This Is Your Life.'

It was a most wonderful warm and moving evening and although she forgave me with a kiss on each cheek, I don't think she will ever trust any more freelance television directors. Come to think of it, neither will her friends.

Every launch of a new James Bond film has its own hype to justify the many millions of pounds spent on each production, and the new film *Goldeneye* was no exception. I was keen, however, not to surprise the new Bond, Pierce Brosnan, but do a *Life* on the 80-year-old Desmond Llewellyn, who had played the character of 'Q' for so many years, the man who provides Bond with all his gadgets.

We researched his life and it proved to be a wonderful story, from his early RADA days to his many films including a part in *Cleopatra*. What was really interesting was the fact that as a soldier in the Second World War he had seen action and was eventually captured and made a prisoner of war for five years. Not only that – he had been actively involved in tunnelling out only to be caught by his German guards.

This is the sort of story that we all love and we wanted to do it when the film came out as a sort of topical peg to hang it from.

Desmond was going to be at the press launch of the film at the Hyde Park Hotel and that was the best time to spring our surprise. I knew that if people saw Michael at the press launch then they would think that we were about to surprise Pierce Brosnan, the star of the film. To stamp out that idea I thought we should have him with Michael at the beginning to help us with springing the 'hit'. This would also tell our audience that Pierce was not our subject that night.

It would also be fun to have a conspiratorial meeting between Michael Aspel and James Bond. We set up a bar and Michael rehearsed the scene with John Graham standing in for Pierce Brosnan, who was arriving off a plane from New York. Within the hour Pierce had arrived and said that if time was tight, he did not need a rehearsal. I showed him the script and took him through the moves and then he simply said: 'Let's do it.'

Michael stood against the bar, the obligatory vodka martini in one hand and the Red Book in the other. He walked over to Pierce, who was sitting at the other end of the bar.

Pierce said: 'You're late, Double O Eight.' Michael replied: 'You said eleven, Double O Seven.'

And so it went on. It was great fun, a perfect take and a

wonderful opening for the programme. Pierce went on to help Michael distract Desmond at the press conference while Michael and the book appeared from the other side.

I wondered why Pierce had put himself to so much trouble; the programme touched on but was not about his film. The answer came when Pierce came on the programme in the studio, and after giving Desmond a great tribute, actually kissed his hand. He was obviously genuinely very fond of this 80-year-old character actor.

Maybe I am getting cynical in my old age but I found this behaviour very moving coming as it did from a very big screen star. Well done to Pierce Brosnan, and long may he reign as 007.

David Essex has the perfect *This Is Your Life* story, with a hard beginning, perseverance and enormous talent that has taken him across several decades from the sixties right up to 1995.

We knew that he had just written all the music for a two-and-a-half hour ice spectacular based on *Beauty and the Beast*. He had also starred in many films and played a leading role as Che Guevara in *Evita*. His was an excellent story, but where could we spring the surprise; he was another person who was not easy to pin down.

Mel Bush was the producer of the show and he told us that David was rehearsing the show with a team of top star Russian ice skaters in Moscow, so did we want to spring our surprise there?

In a flash we were off to Russia for our survey, just to see if it was possible.

After a bleak dark entrance and further cold bureaucracy at Moscow Airport we were finally driven into the centre of Moscow and to our hotel in Red Square. It should have been all very exciting except that I had been to Moscow 25 years before and to me there was a very depressing greyness about the place and the people. This was not helped by the fact that the rehearsals were held in the darkest, bleakest and dirtiest ice rink that I had ever seen.

The team of dancers were young and very exciting, but we just could not shake off the gloom that was surrounding the place. I decided I didn't want to shoot the opening of our programme in such a depressing location.

What about in Red Square? We all trooped off to see it. It was mostly covered in a dull green tarpaulin held by endless scaffolding. If possible, it looked worse than the ice rink.

'What about . . .' The question was never finished because at that moment someone decided to fire a missile at the American Embassy, blasting a hole clean through one of its stone walls. Since the Embassy was only half a mile away at the other end of the square, this did rather disrupt our thoughts at that time. It had cost us many thousands of pounds to survey Moscow but the explosion had made up my mind. Someone is trying to tell us not to do the opening here and I think we should go straight home.

Which is why we found ourselves outside the Albert Hall in London in December 1995, with Michael about to gate-crash the ice rink at the end of *Beauty and the Beast*. The Albert Hall is a spectacular looking place and the interior with its ice stage covered by dazzling lights gave it a magical appearance.

David Essex took his bow from the 3,000-strong audience at the finale and sang one of his numbers from the production. The young dancers in their fantastic costumes applauded with the audience as Michael came on the stage where a special carpet had been laid down by two dancers to say to David Essex: 'This Is Your Life.'

It was a wonderful evening. I think I'll leave Moscow to the politicians and the green scaffolding.

Epilogue

E ven after all these years, with an experienced team around me and the wonders of modern television technology to rely on, things can still go wrong on a show like *This Is Your Life*. We have far more successes than failures but we can still sometimes run into your basic, old-fashioned brick wall that none of our combined talents nor any of our technical resources can get us over, round, through or under.

What, for example, do Anne Diamond, Lennox Lewis and Tony Curtis all have in common? None of them (at the time of writing) have been surprised by Michael Aspel with a Red Book. Another common factor is that they have all been within hours of the programme before I have been forced to cancel everything.

Anne Diamond was to be our subject from her television studio at Pebble Mill in Birmingham. Her live programme, *Good Morning*, with Nick Owen was to be invaded by us just as they were about to finish for that day. Because it was live we arranged with the BBC producer to pretend to wind up the programme some minutes early which would give Michael just enough time to crash the studio and present the book. Anne is a very experienced television person and is, naturally, very conscious of time, so a suitable reason for the underrun had to be invented. Us producers are pretty devious and some network excuse was found.

Another problem was that Anne had placed some insurance

with her very good friend and co-presenter Nick Owen. She made him promise to tell her if he ever found out that we were planning the surprise. Both of them had to be fooled, but some people in the studio just had to know. The cameraman, the floor manager, the production assistant and, of course, the director. In collusion with Anne's husband, Mike Hollingsworth, we were now within 48 hours of the 'hit'.

The journey to Birmingham was arranged with enough cars to get us back to our studios at Teddington in time for the programme. A special route to get into the Pebble Mill studios through a fire exit was set up with a security man in place to open the door at a special time. Michael Aspel, Johnny Graham, Liz Fleming (my P.A.) and myself were on our way to the studios for a last minute, early morning briefing, when I picked up the morning paper to read during the journey.

ANNE DIAMOND TV SURPRISE AT PEBBLE MILL TODAY. The story was running in all the Birmingham papers and had been picked up by the London editions. Someone who had made a few quid for the story had leaked it to a reporter and that was the end of that surprise.

Lennox Lewis was the World Heavyweight Champion and he was to defend his title against Oliver McCall. Now, with all due respect to Mr McCall, he was not expected to last the distance. Everyone predicted that he would be outclassed by Lennox and beaten. It was agreed with his family and boxing advisers that, so easy was this fight, we could actually pull the surprise straight after the bout and do the programme within two hours.

Not a good idea, we thought, because he might get hurt with an unlucky punch. I could not imagine Michael reading the Red Book to two black eyes. It was agreed that we would wait until the press conference on the following morning. The American boxer Marvin Hagler was flown in from Rome and all our guests were to be gathered at the studios at seven o'clock that evening. I thought that it would be a good idea if John Graham and the writer of the programme, Norman Giller, went to the fight that night to see if we could spot any other guests for the programme.

Early the following morning, my telephone rang and Norman Giller told me the impossible news that Lennox Lewis had been beaten and was no longer the reigning World Champion. We all gathered in my office. A decision had to be made within two hours on whether we should do it or not. The press conference was still on and we could still crash in and pull our surprise.

Norman was for it, John was for it and I thought we might get away with it but Michael's instincts told him that a boxer who had just lost his world title would not take kindly to a celebration just at that time. We decided to cancel, but the family still wanted us to go ahead – it would be a consolation prize they thought.

We debated again but were convinced that he would say no and then we and Michael would look like insensitive idiots for even trying. Lennox was a very good boxer and there was no doubt that one day he would bounce back (unfortunate phrase) and then we would be there. So, in spite of a very disappointed family, we stood all the studio crews down and cancelled within a few hours of the production.

When we decided to feature the programme on Bob Hope, who had reached his 92nd year and was still in great form, we also decided to feature Dolores (Mrs Hope). We had the usual problems with trying to tie Bob down to be at a given place at a predictable time, but it was working.

We knew that he would be in Los Angeles for a few weeks so it made sense if we could also do another person whom we had been trying to get for many years. As the Bob Hope programme progressed, we set up another on Tony Curtis. I had met him the year before and I knew he was on very good form. He was also a very serious painter and his exhibitions and sales were world wide. Most importantly, we had the blessing and cooperation from his daughter, actress Jamie Lee Curtis.

Both programmes were now well underway and we made Bob and Dolores Hope's *This Is Your Life* which was a very big success at the CBS studios.

Our happiness was short lived, however, when we heard that Tony had suddenly decided to take some time off and go to paint in Mexico. Worst still, nobody knew where he was going. 'After all,' his agent said, 'he thinks he has a clear week.' All our efforts with contacts in the travel world and with his other friends did not reveal his whereabouts and each of our deadlines came and went ... our time ran out. On our last deadline day I reluctantly accepted a temporary defeat, cancelled the CBS studios and had Mandy Lee, our production manager, rebook all our return air tickets to London. We came home with a superb programme on Bob Hope and empty handed on Tony Curtis.

I say temporary defeat because all three programmes will be done some day in the future when Anne and Lennox and Tony are least expecting it.

We were almost also beaten for another programme by of all things ... a food processor! It had taken over six months to research and set up our *Life* on England cricketer Graham Gooch, but we managed all the hurdles of his changing schedules and overseas trips to finally get him to meet up with some friends for an evening meal in a Surrey hotel before going off for another bash at the Australians in Sydney.

This problem was that we had set up in the reception area of the hotel which had, for some strange reason, very limited electrical facilities for our equipment. We have, of course, special generating equipment of our own but it is very cumbersome and would be easily spotted by Graham. Our technical manager Nigel Spong made an extensive survey of the hotel and was sure that by plugging in some lights in one area and running other cables through into the main kitchen he could run two cameras and our recording machines from their kitchen plugs. I was not convinced, but he made some tests and, sure enough, everything worked.

Graham was on time. His car was spotted by our lookout, who telephoned us to say that he was about ten minutes away. Allowing for him to park, we had fifteen minutes. All was well. Our two cameras were hidden by two six foot potted plants and all our cables were hidden. We had also hidden all of the England cricket team, who were pleased to be able to put something over on Graham for all their own reasons.

Nobody, however, could know which entrance Graham would choose. We tried to persuade the hotel to close the alternative doors but the hotel manager would not even think of it. I was hidden behind an *Evening Standard* at the front reception and Michael was positioned up on the mezzanine floor so he could get to Graham whichever way he came in.

'This is going well,' I foolishly thought. Then the lights went out, along with the power for our tape machines. Apparently, the hotel electrics could cope with our power requirements, but only just. With five minutes to go, someone in the main kitchen switched on a food processor and that was a few watts too far!

Nigel Spong was into the kitchen like a flash, but he did not know where the fuse boxes were. He asked the staff, who were Italian and Spanish, but his gestures were not understood. He opened every door he could find including the hotel deep freeze until he found the box.

Two bits of fuse wire and Thames Television's biggest programme for over fifteen million people was ready to roll again. Michael leapt into action as the lights came back on and Graham Gooch was well and truly 'bowled'.

It was 1956 when *This Is Your Life* started and I took photographs on that first programme as a 24-year-old. Now, in

1996, I have just finished the 27th series. It has spanned a period of 40 years and a total of 1,011 *Lives*. I have produced the programme for over 600 of them and I love to look back at all those surprises, all those near-disasters and all those times when we got it right.

In the main I like to think that a great deal of happiness has been created in the reunions and the tears. It's also my 40th year in television. I must start to grow up soon.

When am I going to stop?

How many jobs do you know where you get paid to go around the world, meet everybody you ever wanted to meet, and have a party every week?

No, don't apply . . . I'm not leaving just yet.

Index

This Is My Life

This Is My Life